ncea business studies

a workbook @ level 3

david farquhar

NCEA Business Studies: a workbook @ Level 3
1st Edition
David Farquhar

Cover design: Book Design Ltd
Text designer: Book Design Ltd
Production controller: Siew Han Ong

Any URLs contained in this publication were checked for currency during the production process. Note, however, that the publisher cannot vouch for the ongoing currency of URLs.

Acknowledgements
Images on pages 7, 8 (centre), 14, 15, 28, 33, 41 42, 44, 63, 68 (the globe), 69, 77, 81, 103, 110, 111, 119, 120, 125 and 128 courtesy of Shutterstock.

Articles on pages 10, 39, 45, 50, 73, 75, 79, 83, 94 and 116 courtesy of the New Zealand Herald.

For product information and technology assistance,
in Australia call **1300 790 853**;
in New Zealand call **0800 449 725**

For permission to use material from this text or product, please email **aust.permissions@cengage.com**

National Library of New Zealand Cataloguing-in-Publication Data
A catalogue record for this book is available from the National Library of New Zealand.

978 0 17 035259 8

Cengage Learning Australia
Level 7, 80 Dorcas Street
South Melbourne, Victoria Australia 3205

Cengage Learning New Zealand
Unit 4B Rosedale Office Park
331 Rosedale Road, Albany, North Shore 0632, NZ

For learning solutions, visit **cengage.co.nz**

Printed in Malaysia by Papercraft.
2 3 4 5 6 7 25 24 23

Contents

Introduction

About the author

David Farquhar was born in Waiouru in the central North Island, and completed the majority of his schooling in Tauranga. Following his degree at the University of Waikato, David moved to Auckland to complete a diploma in teaching with his first teaching assignment at Rotorua Girls' High School. Conscious that he was teaching commerce subjects without any real business experience, David left teaching with the expectation to return to the profession at a later date.

The following two decades saw David working in a variety of roles in some of New Zealand's major corporates, where he developed extensive experience in sales, marketing, strategic management, negotiation, organisational change, leadership and economic sustainability. In addition, David has been involved in associations including Packaging Council of New Zealand, Recycling Operators of New Zealand (Chairperson) and Keep New Zealand Beautiful.

David returned to teaching in 2007 at Rangitoto College and promptly set a goal to grow the subject of Business Studies as a relevant and meaningful subject for students. Successfully building from five Business Studies classes at Rangitoto College in 2007 to 12 classes when he left in 2013, David then moved to be Director of Commerce at Avondale College.

In late 2014, David returned to the corporate world, joining Hewlett Packard (HP) as Education Specialist.

David has three children — Jamie, Melissa and Andrew — who were all educated at Northcote College, and is married to Michelle who currently teaches commerce subjects at Mt Albert Grammar in Auckland. David continues to be involved with Business Studies students through the Young Enterprise Trust and the annual Business Boot Camp he established with Massey University in 2013, plus any opportunity to engage and enthuse students in his role with HP.

Acknowledgements

Thank you to the many teachers who have contributed to this workbook directly or indirectly, particularly Michelle Farquhar, Simon Bioletti, Nathan Hockly, Jude Maurice, Nyssa Poffley, Simon Condon, Megan Mogan, Hayley Johns, Steve Aldhamland, Phil Cowley, Mary Kerrigan, Rhonda Donaldson, Andrew Bramston, Jamie Smith, Robyn Frey, David Hodge and Lesley Mitchell.

And to my children who are my best friends as well, I am proud of you - Jamie, Melissa and Andrew.

Any mistakes in this workbook are mine alone.

Why Business Studies?

The majority of people in the world are required to work in some way or another in order to obtain a standard of living. The choices are to work either for someone else, be it a company, charity/trust, government-funded organisation, or for yourself, as an entrepreneur. In whichever case you find yourself, your knowledge of how businesses work and interact with the wider world will be important to your success.

Level 1 Business Studies is concerned with New Zealand businesses of fewer than 20 employees, which is ideal for introduction to basic concepts.

Level 2 Business Studies is concerned with New Zealand businesses of more than 20 employees with the regional or national significance that allow students to demonstrate understanding of how and why businesses respond to internal factors and the consequences of operational decisions.

Level 3 Business Studies is focused on the learning objective to analyse how and why New Zealand businesses operating in global markets make operational and strategic decisions in response to interacting internal and external factors. This learning objective (8.1 in the Curriculum document) is explored within the context of a New Zealand-registered business connected to students' lives operating in global markets (exporters, importers, New Zealand-owned multinationals). The business can be small, medium or large, but should operate in the global market; for example, a New Zealand fashion designer, a web company, an international transport company, dairy company, or an airline company.

Students are expected to:

3.1   Demonstrate their understanding of the internal operations of a business that operates in a global context.

3.2   Demonstrate their understanding of how a business that operates in a global context responds strategically to external factors.

3.3   Discuss a complex problem (or problems) in a given global business, and apply business knowledge to provide possible solutions and recommendations to address issues.

Students and teachers are therefore encouraged to focus on a few companies that meet these criteria and can be covered in depth across all three standards. However, note that 3.3 examinations will use resource material that the students must refer to and apply their knowledge.

In addition, carefully selecting three or four companies for the year as a class focus will enable students to gain a relevant understanding of issues confronting business and how they may respond. A suggested starting list of New Zealand-registered companies is below:

HP	Beca Group Limited
Progressive Enterprises Limited	Zespri
ANZ Bank	Sanford Ltd
Vodafone	Mainfreight Ltd
BurgerFuel	Fisher & Paykel Ltd
3M	Michael Hill International
Starbucks	Datacom
Air New Zealand	Fonterra

Students are expected to demonstrate understanding of the following business knowledge, concepts and content in describing how a business operating in a global market makes operational and strategic decisions in response to interacting internal/external factors for 3.1 and 3.2. For this they need to build knowledge of business terms and be able to provide examples in a business situation.

ISBN: 9780170352598

unit 1

Demonstrate understanding of how internal factors interact within a business that operates in a global context.

Learning Intention 1: Students are expected to demonstrate understanding of the following business knowledge, concept and content:

Unit 1.1   Innovation — by product, by process; risk and opportunities

Unit 1.2   Innovation — corporate cultures and strategies to encourage innovation

Unit 1.3   Intellectual Property management

Unit 1.4   Quality management

Unit 1.5   Change management

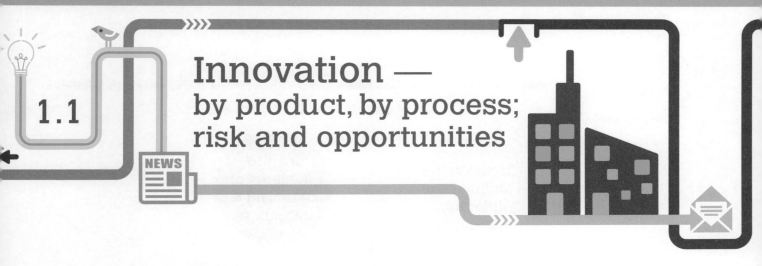

1.1

Innovation —
by product, by process;
risk and opportunities

Innovation is bringing a new idea into being, such as a product for sale (product innovation), or a new way of producing something (process innovation) that creates value for which customers will pay.

To be called an innovation, an idea must come into being at an economical cost and satisfy a specific need. Innovation involves the deliberate application of information, imagination and initiative in deriving values from resources, and includes all processes by which new ideas are generated and converted into useful products or services.

In business, the focus on innovation is seen in the generic term 'research and development' (R&D) — where funds are committed to the generation of new products or processes that will directly benefit the business. Note, however, that the generation of ideas can be from anywhere internally or externally to the business — and the concept of Quality Circles/Lean Manufacturing and Continuous Improvement systems are all methods in which these innovative ideas may be captured. The real test of innovation is how much it contributes to the business — better products, new products, improved production, supply chain or procurement processes, faster communication channels, etc. Students need to consider the role of an innovative culture within a business in Unit 1.2.

The contribution to the business may be through growth (new products, new markets, etc.) and/or increased competitiveness in the market (reduced costs, therefore better able to compete on price).

ISBN: 9780170352598

tasks

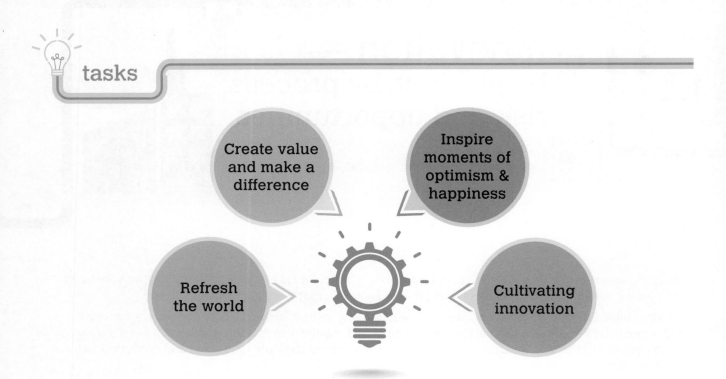

Product innovation	Sustainability innovation	Marketing innovation	System innovation
Where a product is changed (for example adding a feature to a smartphone) or new to the market, such as the HP Sprout. Innovations could be as simple as reducing size or as major as adoption of new technology as in the growth of 'wearable' technology such as Fitbit.	Consumers are increasingly wanting to see firms care for the environment through sustainable use of resources such as through recycling products at the end of their lives. See HP Planet Partners Program for the collection, disassembly and recycling of HP products.	The communication of a product or service has changed dramatically over the past 10 years. No longer does television advertising dominate — now social media, viral marketing, YouTube, etc. all play a part. From a business telling consumers what they want, the movement has shifted to consumers telling businesses what they want.	What culture of innovation exists within the business? Do management and staff have a process to encourage new ideas and the adoption of new techniques to maintain or improve the business's competitiveness? Doing the same thing year after year usually results in stagnation and ultimately the decline of the business.

1   You have been asked by your Chief Executive Officer (CEO) to outline to staff the need for innovation. Identify the four key points you would make to encourage staff involvement.

_____

_____

_____

_____

_____

   ISBN: 9780170352598

2   For each of your four points in 1, provide examples of innovation from a real business you have studied and its importance to the sustainability of that business.

_____

_____

_____

_____

_____

3   Research the value of 'research and development' expenditure of Sweden, New Zealand, Greece and the United States as a percentage of GDP. The Data section at www.worldbank.org might help you. Suggest reasons for the expenditure of Sweden compared with the other countries. What could you infer from the data as a lesson for New Zealand?

_____

_____

_____

_____

4   Explain briefly, with a real-life example, what product innovation is.

_____

_____

_____

5   Explain briefly, with a real-life example, what process innovation is.

_____

_____

_____

6   Outline the relationship between an organisational culture and an innovation culture. Use examples where possible. After completing your answer, discuss with other class members and develop a number of real-life examples that you could quote in an exam.

_____

_____

_____

_____

_____

7 NCEA-style question.

Child's sores cured by doctor 360 km away

Eight-year-old David Tautari has finally got treatment for nasty sores on his leg, thanks to a photo emailed to a doctor 360 km away.

David, a Year 4 pupil at Pukekohe North School, first got sores on his leg when he visited Whangarei at Christmas time, and new sores flared up again recently.

They were finally picked up last week when the decile 1 school joined an experimental 'tele-medicine' scheme run by Kaitaia's Dr Lance O'Sullivan, which already serves 17 remote schools in the Far North.

Trained volunteers use an iPad app to send a photo of children with skin infections to Dr O'Sullivan's clinic in Kaitaia. Dr O'Sullivan or a colleague assesses the infection and sends a prescription if required to the nearest pharmacy.

Pukekohe North principal Robyn Withers-Lauer said the scheme found 41 of the school's 190 students had untreated skin infections in its first week.

a Use an example from the resource above to explain the term 'product innovation' in regard to the services offered by the clinic.

_____

_____

_____

_____

b Fully explain ONE reason why being innovative is important for Dr O'Sullivan's clinic's long-term growth. Include reference to the benefits to society of this innovation by the clinic.

_____

_____

_____

_____

_____

_____

_____

8 NCEA-style question.

The CEO of a local health board recently attended a conference on innovation in health care. The speaker at the conference suggested that three strategies are essential if a culture of innovation is to be developed and sustained in an organisation:

1 Rewarding risk-taking

2 Tolerating mistakes

3 Insisting on open communication.

The CEO was not convinced, as risk-taking and making mistakes could lead to serious harm to people needing care.

 ISBN: 9780170352598

Select ONE strategy from the blue box on page 10, or any other strategy suitable for a New Zealand business operating in global markets. Evaluate whether the implementation of the selected strategy is likely to result in a health board or health provider achieving a culture that supports innovation. In your answer:

a   Fully explain ONE positive and ONE negative impact that the implementation of the selected strategy may have on the culture of the health board or provider.

_____

_____

_____

_____

b   Provide a justified conclusion as to whether the implementation of the selected strategy is likely to result in the health board or provider achieving a culture that supports innovation.

Selected strategy: _____

_____

_____

_____

_____

_____

_____

_____

_____

_____

_____

_____

_____

example

3M NZ

3M is a diversified technology company serving customers and communities with innovative products and services. In 2010, sales were in excess of $26 billion worldwide. Each of its five businesses has earned leading global market positions; it is this breadth of experience and product lines that provides them with the ability to serve customers locally here in New Zealand, providing solutions in response to their specific customer needs.

In New Zealand, 3M employs approximately 140 staff in technical, accounting, sales, marketing and many other specialist roles. 3M has a tradition of innovation, which has become part of their ethos and their everyday business-life. The 3M focus on efficiency through continuous improvement, strong presence in the industrial, commercial, healthcare and consumer markets, combined with an ongoing flow of new products, and collaboration with its customers has the company well positioned for sustainable growth in the future.

tasks

9　a　Research the following 3M brands and identify the innovation involved.

Brand	Innovation
Command Strips	
Post-it Notes	
Scotch Tapes	
Scotch-Brite scourers	
Scotchgard	
Nexcare bandages/ plasters	

b　Which of the above products has a sustainability feature? That is, is recyclable, reusable, or longer lasting than competitors' products?

_____

_____

_____

_____

_____

c　Visit the 3M USA website, www.3m.com, for evidence of innovation. Visit the Newsroom for stories. Identify and describe a key innovation that the company has announced in the past 12 months.

_____

_____

_____

d   What does the website say about the role of innovation as a feature for the success and sustainability of the company? Explain with reference to an example.

_____

_____

_____

_____

_____

e   Trivial question: What does 3M stand for? (Clue: it's a short version of the full name of the company.)

_____

_____

10 In 2015, Microsoft released Windows 10. Visit the company website, www.microsoft.com, and answer the following questions.

a   Why is there no Windows 9?

_____

_____

b   How was Windows 10 developed differently than all previous versions of Microsoft? (Hint: Windows Insider.)

_____

_____

_____

c   Describe three features of Windows 10 that you would classify as innovative and why.

i   _____

_____

ii   _____

_____

iii _____

_____

d   Windows 10 was released as a free upgrade for Windows 7 and 8 users. What was the 'normal' method of upgrading the operating system? Is this innovative, and if so by what method as per the diagram on page 8?

_____

_____

_____

_____

_____

_____

1.2 Innovation — corporate cultures and strategies to encourage innovation

As developed in the last unit, innovation refers to:

'Bringing a new idea into being, such as a product for sale (product innovation), or a new way of producing something (process innovation) that creates value or for which customers will pay.'

We will now incorporate this idea into the corporate culture of a business, and the importance of strategies to encourage innovation.

Corporate Culture (sometimes referred to as Organisational Culture)

The corporate culture is the values, attitudes, beliefs and behaviours that contribute to the environment of an organisation and influences how people interact with each other both internally and externally. It can be summed up as 'the way we do things around here' and 'what is normal' for that organisation.

Corporate culture includes an organisation's expectations, experiences, philosophy and values, and is shown in its self-image, staff relationships, interactions with the outside world, and future expectations. It is based on shared attitudes, beliefs, customs, and written and unwritten rules that have been developed over time and are considered valid.

Examples include:

1 the way the organisation conducts its business (ethics), treats its employees, customers and the wider community

2 the extent to which freedom is allowed in decision-making, developing new ideas, and personal expression

3 how influence and information flow through the levels of authority in a business

4 how committed employees are towards the collective objectives of the business.

 ISBN: 9780170352598

It affects the organisation's productivity and performance, and provides guidelines on customer care and service, product quality and safety, attendance and punctuality, and concern for the environment. It also extends to production methods, marketing and advertising practices, and to new product creation. The corporate culture is unique for every organisation and can be one of the hardest things to change.

For example, one school may have a culture that focuses on exam results, while another school may focus on sporting achievement or a balance of sport/academic and arts.

In business, the focus may be on achieving market share at all costs including the acceptance of a high staff turnover compared with another business that may have as a priority retaining staff to build experience.

example

Examples of interesting corporate culture that you should examine include:

Why is it important?

When employees **share** the values, goals, beliefs and behaviours of the business, they will work together as a team. This in turn may promote staff loyalty and motivation to do well, which may result in more sharing of ideas and efficient ways of doing things. The team approach ('there is no "I" in "team"') is very similar to the drive for success in a team sport such as the All Blacks or the school netball team. Every great team reviews its performance, and members motivate each other to find ways to improve either their own performance, the department they operate within the business or the whole business.

tasks

1   As a class, try to capture the organisational culture of the school you attend. What is the school's attitude to quality (academic/sporting/cultural results, leadership roles, environmental issues) and improving performance? Can you identify five innovations in process or product (the student outcomes) at the school in the last two years?

_____

_____

_____

_____

_____

_____

2   What teams operate within the school? Create a bubble map in the space provided of the various teams and label each bubble with the members, such as students/teachers/management. Don't forget to include the wider school teams (e.g. BOT, PTA).

_____

_____

_____

_____

_____

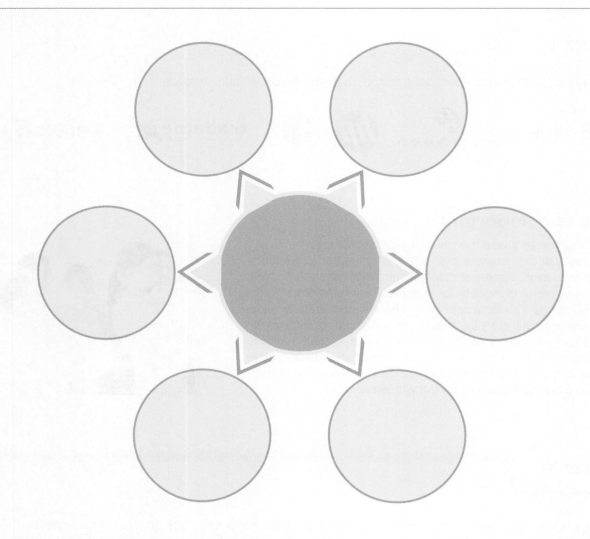

3   Identify the business you would most want to work for if you could start work there next week. What are the characteristics that would attract you? Why?

_____

_____

_____

_____

_____

_____

   ISBN: 9780170352598

The role of innovation

The business that stands still is usually doomed to failure — overtaken in the market by more progressive companies that have brought better products and services to the market at lower prices or at better value to the consumer. Consider the following key businesses that are no longer operating, as they did not adapt to the changing business landscape. In most cases, the corporate culture did not allow the generation of new ideas and the commitment to implement the changes required. 'The way we do things around here' became out of date and therefore the business became uncompetitive.

task

4 a Where have they gone? Research the following companies and find out what happened. List the principal reason for failure.

Business	Reason for failure
BORDERS.	
PAN AM	
COMPAQ	
D▴E▴K▴A Better **value**, every day.	

ISBN: 9780170352598

ENRON ®	
CROWN LYNN NEW ZEALAND	
SEGA ®	
Leed TRADEMARK REGD.	
ARTHURANDERSEN	

b **Innovation**

From the table presented in Task **4a**, choose two companies and suggest how innovation may have kept those companies successful today. For example, what innovation has happened in the airline industry over the past five years regarding services, price, loyalty programmes, food, luggage, destinations, etc.?

_____

_____

_____

 ISBN: 9780170352598

_____

_____

_____

_____

_____

c Research YouTube for what are considered to be the best places to work. Examples include Google, Microsoft, 3M and many more. Why? What features of these companies would you consider drives people to be innovative? List four key elements that management should adopt to encourage a culture of innovation.

_____

_____

_____

_____

_____

_____

d What are the consequences of NOT being innovative? In the space provided, fully explain to a Year 11 Business Studies student the impact on a business.

_____

_____

_____

_____

_____

_____

What is a strategy?

Having accepted that the corporate (or organisational) culture can impact on the performance of a business, then we need to look at the **strategies** to encourage innovation that will result in success or failure of a business.

A **strategy** is a plan of action for the whole organisation that is designed to achieve a particular goal, such as increased sales, increased market share or lower environmental impact.

In simple terms, a **corporate strategy** is working out 'how to get from where we are now to where we want to be in XX years in the future'. From this corporate strategy, the business will develop tactics to get there. A **tactic** is a short-term policy or decision to achieve a step towards the corporate strategy. Typically, a business will have one or two major strategic goals and several tactics to get there.

For example, the corporate strategy could be to reduce the company's environmental impact. A tactic could be to switch all company vehicles from petrol to electric within two years.

How can a business encourage innovation?

Let's examine the barriers to innovation that are most common in a business.

Business activity	Business decision	Is the decision strategic or tactical?	Explanation of why strategic or tactical
Supermarket	Widen product range to include washing machines, vacuum cleaners, and fridges.		
Video shop	Develop in-shop gaming PCs with 32 inch screens for online competitions.		
Holiday tour business	Increase prices in school holidays to most popular destinations		
Health food manufacturer	Develop its own beer brand.		
Computer manufacturer	Develop a range of baseball caps with built-in cameras, GPS and internet capability.		
Dairy farm	Convert to beef farming.		
Clothing retailer	Close all provincial stores and focus on developing online sales.		

Barriers to innovation in a business

Aspect	Possible barrier	Evidence of barrier	Possible solution
Understanding the market	Only using your own market information.	'We can only rely on our own information we gathered.'	Encourage collaboration across all areas of the business. Share resources and information. Foster networking among staff outside their own departments. Interpret data and share across departments and/or give business wide briefings.
	Centralisation	'We will base our decision on our sales data only. What other departments know is irrelevant.'	
	Not co-ordinated across company.	'Takes too long for a decision. We have to talk to so many people.'	
	Myopia	'We have always done it this way. Bigger businesses have that concern, not us.'	
Market knowledge	Over-reliance on a single source of information (such as sales numbers).	'Marketing should have the information on the market, not us.'	Encourage everyone to collect information about the market (sales data, complaints, compliments, demographic, advertising, etc.) and feed it into a central store where everyone can access and analyse it. Staff training on how every interaction with a customer/ supplier or competitor *is* market information, and important to the business.
	No processing of information gathered.	'We have a report we have prepared with all that information – what else is needed?'	
	Belief that the business has all the information it needs already.	'We already have a strategy based on our information. Why should we change?'	
Using market knowledge	Having the information but not really using it or understanding it.	'Our strategy is based on market information, but I am not sure where it's come from.'	Use what information the business has, and make decisions based on it. Formulate trends based on the data, and revisit those trends every six months to see if they are still valid. Question the data. Where did it come from? How old is it? Who actually gathered it, and is it reliable?
	Someone else's issue.	'We talk about the market, so we must have information on it.'	

ISBN: 9780170352598

tasks

5   The organisational culture can often be shaped by the management style demonstrated in the workplace. The most common styles are:

-   autocratic (or authoritarian)
-   democratic
-   paternalistic
-   laissez-faire.

Find the definitions for these styles, and complete the table with two examples for each style. One example from your school or an organisation you know personally, and another example from business/movies, etc. For example, a grammar school principal was traditionally an autocratic manager/leader, and in a movie it would be Robert de Niro in *Men of Honour* or Jack Nicholson in *A Few Good Men*. A female equivalent would be Meryl Streep in *The Devil Wears Prada*.

Definition of styles	Example 1	Example 2
Autocratic (or authoritarian)		
Democratic		
Paternalistic		

Laissez-faire		

6   In small groups, consider the positive and negative impacts of the four management styles on organisations under the following topics:

- Communication within the organisation
- Loyalty and commitment to the organisation
- Innovation
- Recruitment
- Customer focus.

	Autocratic	Democratic	Paternalistic	Laissez-faire
Communication within the organisation				
Loyalty and commitment to the organisation				

ISBN: 9780170352598

Innovation			
Recruitment			
Customer focus			

7   NCEA-style question.

Melissa was a young entrepreneur who had designed a new way of creating small gourmet meals that could be reheated to restaurant quality due to a type of sealed bag system. The bag controlled the moisture content of the food and balanced the ingredients when heated in a microwave. Market research had indicated a strong desire for the product from busy executives with dietary requirements. However, Melissa thinks she needs input from staff on how to formulate the meals, then package the bags in a high-volume production line.

   ISBN: 9780170352598

Evaluate the strategies that Melissa could introduce to make the production side of her company more innovative. In your answer, you should:

- explain TWO strategies she could implement that would encourage workers to develop new ideas
- fully explain the impact of these strategies on the company by explaining ONE positive and ONE negative impact of each strategy on the performance of the business
- draw a justified conclusion as to which strategy would be the more effective.

_____

_____

_____

_____

_____

_____

_____

_____

_____

_____

_____

_____

_____

_____

_____

_____

_____

_____

_____

_____

_____

_____

_____

_____

_____

_____

_____

_____

ISBN: 9780170352598

1.3 Intellectual Property management

What is Intellectual Property?

Intellectual Property (IP) is an umbrella term for human innovations that are protected under national law and international treaties. IP includes a range of commercial assets from patents for new inventions through to copyright-protected artworks.

Developing and managing IP allows a business to align and focus its operations and enhance its competitiveness. IP protection helps in:

- preventing competitors from copying or closely imitating a business's products, technical processes, or business services
- avoiding wasteful investment in research and development and marketing
- creating a corporate identity through a branding strategy
- negotiating licensing, franchising, and other IP-based contractual agreements
- increasing the market value of the business
- acquiring venture capital and enhancing access to finance.

The value of protecting your property

- It is always worthwhile considering the commercial potential of your intellectual property — even though the potential may not be obvious to you right now. For example, when you start a business, you may not consider your business name or logo to be of great value; you may think the 'branding' is only of interest to larger organisations. But from your first day of trading your unique branding helps to establish your reputation in the market place and promote customer recognition of your products or services. Over time, your branding can become a business asset that may substantially increase the value of your business. Consider the brands of Coke, Nike, Ferrari and Ford.
- Also, if you need to secure investment funding at any stage, investors will be interested in the steps you have taken to secure your intellectual property. The level of protection can make your business more valuable by creating barriers to competition and enhance the sustainability of your business.

Some mistaken beliefs about IP rights

Doesn't my business or trading name automatically give me protection?

- It's a common mistake to think that forming a company or securing a domain name automatically gives you the exclusive right to use 'your' name for branding. The best way to get nationwide protection for a new brand/ trademark is to formally register your trademark and logo with the Intellectual Property Office of New Zealand (IPONZ).

 ISBN: 9780170352598

Don't I own the rights to any intellectual property I create?

- With the exception of copyright protection, which is automatic, you must register your rights to gain the benefit from legal protection. You may need to register your rights in several categories, for example design rights can help protect the outward appearance of a product you design, but *not* its function. Patent rights cover the function and purpose of a product.

Key terms

Patent:

A **patent** is an exclusive right granted by the Government for a new invention. The owner of the patent may then exclude others from commercialising the patented invention for up to 20 years. It must be new, inventive and useful. It cannot be obvious to someone with a good knowledge and experience of the subject. It must be capable of being made and used in some kind of industry.

Copyright: Ⓒ

The term 'copyright' refers to a bundle of exclusive rights given to owners of original works like prototype drawings, films and sound recordings. In New Zealand, copyright is an automatic unregistered right that comes into existence every time an original work is created, published and performed.

How long does copyright protection last?

Copyright has a limited legal time of existence. The New Zealand time limit will depend on the original work and when it was either created, published, performed or, in the case of product designs, commercialised.

Copyright work	New Zealand time limit
Literary, dramatic, musical and artistic* works	50 years beyond the death of the author
Publisher's copyright	25 years from publication
Sound recordings and film	50 years from the year in which the work was made
Communication works including repeats	50 years from the initial broadcast or transmission
* Commercialised product designs (artistic work that has been applied industrially) — product designs — works of craftsmanship	 16 years 25 years

ISBN: 9780170352598

Trademark: **TM**

A **trademark** is a unique identifier, often referred to as a 'brand' or 'logo'. Once a trademark is **registered**, the ® symbol may be used with the trademark.

Trademarks can include words, logos, colours, shapes, sounds, smells — or any combination of these. Two examples of commonly recognised trademarks are shown below — they have become valuable assets for the business that registered them:

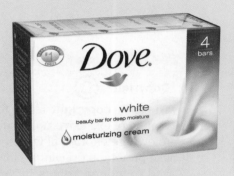 

What are trademarks for?

A trademark means businesses can distinguish their products or services from similar products or services offered by competitors. A carefully selected and managed trademark can become a valuable business asset. As customers learn to value and trust a trademark, they may be willing to pay more for a product or service bearing that mark. For example, if two white T-shirts are on display for sale, with the only difference being one has a swoosh tick on the front......which one would be able to be sold at a higher price? Which one does 'the brand' persuade some buyers to spend more on?

IP management

To survive and grow, all entrepreneurs and business organisations need to know how to protect, manage and exploit their IP assets, and avoid any possible conflict with the IP rights of others. A well-managed IP means IP assets such as a well-known trademark or a market-leading patent can be worth more than the physical company assets. Income for the business can be generated through:

*   the licensing, sale and commercialisation of the IP-protected products, processes or services
*   using the IP to attract business investors, suppliers or outlets and customers or to raise capital.

Without patents and other IP protection:

*   others can copy a successful innovation at minimal cost
*   the original inventor or creator may not receive any financial benefits
*   a business can be beaten by competitors that are in a better position to commercialise the product or process at a more affordable price or volume, or can get to market faster.

tasks

1 Visit the IPONZ website, www.iponz.govt.nz, to answer the following questions.

  a What is the fee for a provisional specification for a patent?

  _____

  b What is the fee for a complete specification for a patent?

  _____

  c What is the annual renewal fee?

  _____

  d What is the expected timeframe for a complete specification application to be completed?

  _____

2 While in Year 13, three of your friends have been working on an app that will cross reference data to match movie preferences, fast food preferences and geolocation data. What advice would you give your friends regarding protection of their app?

  _____

  _____

  _____

  _____

  _____

3 Find out who holds the patent for two of the following products and when; also check what court battles have resulted from these patents:

  Band-Aid   **Aspirin**   **Bluetooth**   **MP3**   **Gumboots**   **Ballpoint pen**

  _____

  _____

  _____

  _____

  _____

  _____

  _____

  _____

  _____

4   NCEA-style question.

Use the information in the box below, and your business knowledge, to answer this question.

> Amanda's Party Apps (APA) is keen to release entertainment software that mixes latest hit music with new smart lighting systems, but is aware that intellectual property theft is very common. The marketing director has consulted an intellectual property lawyer, who is currently investigating the appropriate intellectual property protection for APA's entertainment product. The lawyer has suggested that APA will also need intellectual property protection over some of its other intangible assets, such as its trademark and branding. The lawyer is particularly interested in investigating protection for the APA logo to prevent unauthorised copying.

a   Discuss the importance of APA using trademarks as a form of intellectual property protection. In your answer:

   •   explain the term 'intellectual property'
   •   use an example to fully explain how APA would benefit from a trademark to protect its intellectual property.

_____

_____

_____

_____

_____

_____

_____

_____

_____

_____

_____

_____

_____

_____

_____

_____

_____

b   Evaluate the likely outcomes for a New Zealand firm operating in a global context that you have studied in depth, of an investment in international intellectual property protection, *other than a patent*. This could be an investment in international intellectual property protection that has happened previously, or may happen in the future. In your answer:

   •   select the type of intellectual property protection the company has used, or may use
   •   fully explain ONE positive and ONE negative outcome of the company obtaining the selected intellectual property protection on a global level
   •   draw a justified conclusion as to whether the purchase of the intellectual property protection by the firm would be likely to lead to improved long-term performance.

Name of New Zealand registered business:

_____

Response:

_____
_____
_____
_____
_____
_____
_____
_____
_____
_____
_____
_____
_____
_____
_____
_____
_____
_____
_____
_____

Goods sold or service provided:

_____
_____
_____
_____
_____
_____
_____
_____
_____

ISBN: 9780170352598

Type of intellectual property protection:

ISBN: 9780170352598

Quality management

What is the difference between Quality Assurance and Quality Control?

Quality Control (QC): An aspect of the quality assurance process that consists of detection and measurement of the variability of output due to the production system, and includes corrective responses.

Quality Assurance (QA): Often used interchangeably with quality control, it is a **wider concept** that covers **all policies and systematic activities implemented within a quality system**, including:

1 establishing parameters of adequate technical requirement of inputs and outputs

2 certification and rating of suppliers

3 testing of procured material for its conformance to established quality, performance, safety and reliability standards

4 proper receipt, storage and issue of material

5 audit of the process

6 review of the process to establish required changes

7 audit of the final output for conformance to requirements.

The difference is quality control is concerned with actions to measure the quality of the output, be it a service or product. So it is inspecting, measuring, sampling, etc. Quality assurance is quality control plus a lot more — checking qualifications of suppliers, ensuring defective output from one section of production does not get passed on to the next stage, design of the product to meet customers' needs, delivery systems to customer or market, after-sales service.

Relevance to a business

Quality control takes time and resources as inspections occur, and often the product or service has already been produced to a point where the rejection based on quality has impacts on waste. For example, the inspection of a toy at the warehouse — all production costs up to this point will be a waste if a defect is found. Quality assurance often has inspections and control systems built into the production system so defects are caught early, corrected and therefore waste minimised. For quality assurance, there is almost no need for a final inspection, as every element along the production chain has been inspected and meets quality standards.

ISBN: 9780170352598

Quality Control: checking or inspecting during the production process, often at the last stage, e.g. pass/fail.

Quality Assurance: checking before production (suppliers, staff, utilities), during production, at the end of production, and after sale (warranty service).

Kaizen, Lean production, and Total Quality Management (TQM)

Kaizen is a Japanese term that basically means continuous improvement, and it is largely attributed to the success of the Japanese car industry over the American car industry. In kaizen, the focus is workers meeting regularly to identify ways to improve through small steps the efficiency of the production process. The small steps are often low cost and immediately effective based on the workers recognising better ways in which to carry out their work. The American car industry, in general, would look to large-scale ways to improve efficiency, such as the construction of a new production facility, which would be **high cost and time consuming**. The diagram below illustrates how the two systems both led to productivity improvements, with the advantage of kaizen being that **smaller improvements often will yield positive improvements at low cost.** Another feature of kaizen is the retaining of skilled employees, whereas the construction of a new production facility may result in mass redundancies at an older facility.

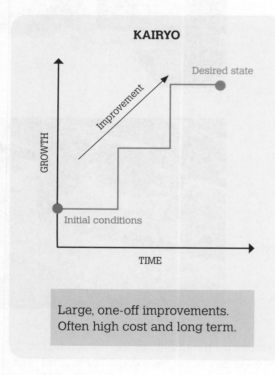

Large, one-off improvements. Often high cost and long term.

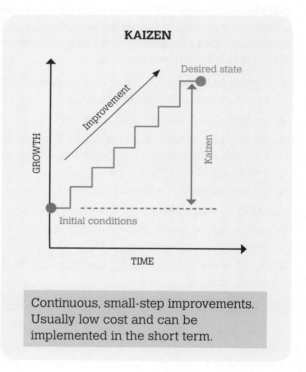

Continuous, small-step improvements. Usually low cost and can be implemented in the short term.

One important aspect already mentioned is where workers meet regularly to suggest improvements. These scheduled meetings were known as quality circles and became a feature of kaizen/continuous improvement systems.

 ISBN: 9780170352598

Lean production is a method of production that focuses on the elimination of waste. While this may seem obvious, as waste can be seen as a cost in terms of wasted packaging, electricity and components, its real value is identifying **time as a waste**. For example, a business may calculate it will take four weeks to deliver a product to a customer. Close analysis might show that at various stages in producing the product it sits around waiting for a further process of production (such as sitting one week in a warehouse before delivery to a customer).

Lean production makes the business look at its production flow and work out a way to produce the same product and deliver to the customer in the shortest time frame possible. **Why?** Because time literally costs money to a business, as every second the product takes to get to the customer delays when payment for the product will occur.

Delays in delivery may be caused through checking and rechecking of the product, which would appear to be a focus on quality. However, if the good is made perfect first time every time then checking and rechecking becomes a time-wasting activity and can be eliminated.

Total Quality Management (TQM) is a process where a business has every employee concerned with quality. One method is to consider whoever you work for **as a customer**, including other employees. In this case, you ensure quality is at 100% as the product leaves your station to go to the next (your co-worker's) station/stage of production.

Quality circles play a key role, as employees will look at suggestions to improve quality as a positive rather than a criticism in a focus on producing a product right the first time every time. Hence the importance of organisational culture within a business — is it quality focused or profit focused?

Two criticisms of TQM are how long the process may take to convince every employee of the importance of quality, and for management to initiate the changes suggested by employees in a timely manner. When the suggested changes from employees are not carried out, employees will lose faith in the system and cease contributing improvement ideas, which eventually results in a loss of quality.

All these methods are aimed at reducing costs, increasing efficiency and therefore making the business more competitive.

Reminder: Economies of scale

These are the factors that lead to a reduction in unit cost as a business increases its operation. For example, if a business should double its output, but the increasing costs are less than double, the cost per unit of producing that output decreases. Simply, as a firm increases its output, it would be expected to capture decreased costs per unit produced, which is economies of scale.

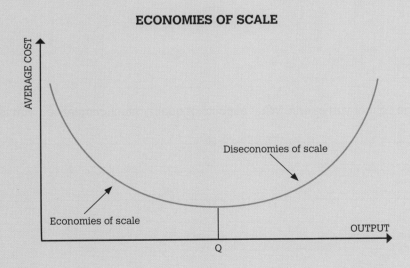

ECONOMIES OF SCALE

ISBN: 9780170352598

tasks

1   Consider the following statement:

'Quality management will increase the quality of production. This may raise revenue as sales increase/costs decrease, as fewer goods are returned because of faults due to poor quality.'

With reference to any business making a product (YES activity, case study you have looked at, or a business you are aware of), expand this statement to include examples and expected real-life situations.

_____

_____

_____

_____

_____

_____

2   With reference to a business you know, explain the importance of Total Quality Management to that business. Ensure you define TQM as part of your answer and clarify 'importance' in regard to profit, output, waste or customers (all or at least one).

_____

_____

_____

_____

_____

3   Have a look at the school you attend. What aspects of quality management can you identify?

_____

_____

_____

_____

_____

_____

_____

4   You have been asked to present to the CEO on the importance of economies of scale. Suggest three reasons why economies of scale could directly improve the sustainability of a business.

_____

_____

_____

_____

_____

_____

_____

_____

5   Consider one of the major fast food businesses operating in your area such as McDonald's, Burger King, KFC, Pita Pit or Subway. In groups or pairs, develop a star chart of the main operational areas of the business such as marketing, production, finance, human resources, management. Choose two of these areas and identify and explain how quality improvements and/or failures would impact on the business.

Quality issue 1	Quality issue 2

_____

_____

_____

_____

_____

ISBN: 9780170352598   PHOTOCOPYING OF THIS PAGE IS RESTRICTED UNDER LAW.

6 Find the definition of each term below and provide a clear example of where this can be seen in a business you have studied or discussed in class.

a Just-in-time manufacturing:

b Automation:

c Mechanisation:

d Piecework:

e Six Sigma:

 ISBN: 9780170352598

7   Quality and product recalls

a   Visit www.consumeraffairs.govt.nz and read the current alerts for products that are required to be withdrawn from the public. In particular, look at the information on the recall of the 'Inside Out' movie novelty souvenir beverage cup.

German order triggers recall of 8.5M VW cars in Europe

BERLIN (AP) German authorities on Thursday ordered a recall of all Volkswagen cars fitted with emissions test-cheating software, a decision that will affect 8.5 million VW diesel vehicles across the 28-nation European Union.

The Federal Motor Transport Authority announced that the recall would affect 2.4 million vehicles in Germany. Under EU rules, cars that are cleared in one country are automatically approved across the bloc, so the repeal also affects Volkswagen vehicles elsewhere in the Union.

Volkswagen said in a statement that it would approach customers, who can already enter their car's serial number on a special website to find out whether it is affected. Apart from the company's VW brand, Audi, SEAT and Skoda cars can also be checked.

The fix will be free for customers, it said.

Also on Thursday, US environmental regulators said they expect to get a proposed fix from Volkswagen next week on about 90,000 of the 482,000 cars with the cheating software in the US. The fix must be tested before the US Environmental Protection Agency will seek a recall. It's unclear when the remaining US cars would be fixed.

In Germany, Transport Minister Alexander Dobrindt said Volkswagen would have to present replacement software for certain cars that have a 2.0 liter diesel engine this month and begin fitting vehicles with them next year.

'VW is ordered ... to remove the software from all vehicles and to take appropriate measures to ensure that the emissions rules are fulfilled,' Dobrindt told reporters in Berlin.

Dobrindt refrained from publicly criticizing Volkswagen, saying cooperation with the German automaker was 'extraordinarily good'.

Asked about German media reports that more than two dozen Volkswagen managers had been suspended by the company amid signs that knowledge of the defect devices was widespread, Dobrindt said his ministry had 'no information about who decided where, when at Volkswagen about the use of such software'.

Volkswagen has said around 11 million cars with the software were sold worldwide, 2.8 million of them in Germany. Dobrindt said only 2.4 million Volkswagen diesel cars with the software are still registered in Germany.

b   i   Does VW have a quality issue? Explain your answer.

_____

_____

_____

_____

_____

_____

ii   What strategic approach has VW management made in regard to the issue?

_____

_____

_____

_____

_____

_____

_____

iii   Explain what some of the consequences are of this issue to the larger VW business, including its other brands.

_____

_____

_____

_____

_____

_____

_____

_____

_____

_____

_____

_____

Change management

In business, change is inevitable. New products, technology, materials, and changing consumer preferences, tastes and incomes. Add into the mix changing political factors such as government regulations (tax, health and safety regulations, tariffs/subsidies), the 'normal' competitive pressures of providing goods and services into a market, and change management becomes one of the key critical factors for the sustainability of a business.

Change management is the planning, implementing, controlling and reviewing of the movement of an organisation from its current state to a new one, while minimising resistance to the change through the involvement of key players and stakeholders.

Consider a business that senior management decides should have a greater focus on environmental issues, and therefore will only accept raw materials from a sustainable source, which is consequently at a higher cost, and which may flow through to the retail price and ultimately its competitiveness. The resulting change may be more acceptable to consumers, but will they accept the higher price relative to other products on the market? If sales are not as strong, what will be the future impact on the business output, on staffing levels, on the firm's ability to fund marketing campaigns, or to negotiate to purchase from suppliers competitively?

Change management factors can be internal or external, or a mixture of both. Internal change management may come about due to moving from a quality control system to a TQM focus, or a restructure. External change management may come from venturing into new markets globally or new government regulations on health and safety requirements. Some of these changes may impact internally and externally, such as the need to redesign a product (internally) to meet external legal requirements such as packaging or point of sale.

Change can also be gradual, including improving economic welfare, or dramatic such as a war or oil price rise or collapse (both situations occurred with oil over the past five years).

We will focus on *internal* change management in this section.

Note: Teachers may want to explore the following key theorists on change management models. Students do not need more than one model to help explain change management, provided students relate the model to the business case presented.

*   Elizabeth Kubler-Ross: http://www.mycvandme.co.uk/blog/the-kubler-ross-change-curve.html. This model was used in the 2013 NCEA exam, question 3, page 10.
*   Kotter's 8-Step Change Model: http://www.kotterinternational.com/the-8-step-process-for-leading-change/
*   Kurt Lewin's three-stage model of organisational change: http://www.change-management-coach.com/kurt_lewin.html

---

Whichever model you choose, the key aspects will include recognising the major causes of change. Note the models suggested often deal with involvement of stakeholders. An alternative method of change management is 'top down' — where senior management dictates the changes including when, what and how with little or no stakeholder involvement. This style often is direct, fast and can create a culture of distrust between stakeholders, which can impact on business performance. Top down change management is often linked with an autocratic management style.

Any of the following external factors will impact *internally* on the business.

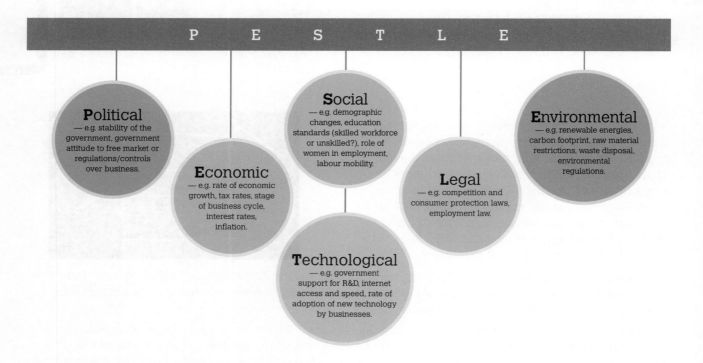

Let's try to apply PESTLE to our change management models in the following case studies.

case study 1

Heaven's Pizza

Andrew Polo runs a successful pizza business called Heaven's Pizza, employing 20 full-time staff and 25 part-timers. He has four locations across New Zealand, and is looking at establishing a franchise model in Australia and eventually Europe, having seen the success of Burger Fuel. However, lately the business has been hit with the following issues:

- Rising import costs of some ingredients due to falling New Zealand exchange rate compared with the US dollar, and higher fuel costs for deliveries.
- Increased Kiwisaver contributions by employers announced by Government.
- Increase in minimum wage.
- Need for new EFTPOS facilities due to credit card fraud.
- Discussion by councils about waste food items being donated to charities rather than thrown away.
- Society wanting gluten-free and low-fat pizzas as obesity levels in New Zealand rise.

 ISBN: 9780170352598

Categorise these factors into the PESTLE model and link them directly to operational issues for Heaven's Pizza. An example has been done for you.

PESTLE category	External factor	Operational issue for Heaven's Pizza
Political		
Economic	Higher cost of fuel due to exchange rate	High costs for deliveries
Social		
Technological		
Legal		
Enviromental		

Now take an operational issue and work though a change management strategy for the business. For example: using the higher cost of deliveries, the business might decide to only make deliveries within certain time periods such as 6 p.m. to 10 p.m. This will impact on costs — fewer staff (part-time drivers) needed outside these hours, so labour costs decrease. With fewer deliveries, there may also be reduced fuel costs. If there are to be fewer part-time staff, the business could decide to discuss with all staff the need for fewer staff. Staff will initially be in denial — that the issue won't affect them or it's other people's fault.

Kubler-Ross curve applied to business change

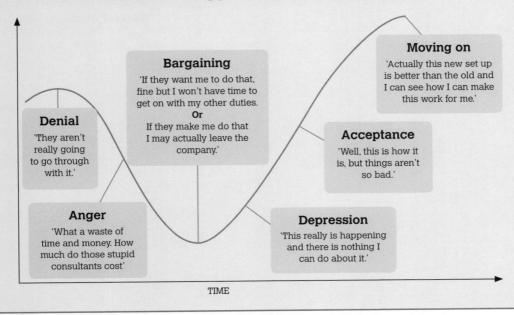

Denial
'They aren't really going to go through with it.'

Anger
'What a waste of time and money. How much do those stupid consultants cost'

Bargaining
'If they want me to do that, fine but I won't have time to get on with my other duties.
Or
If they make me do that I may actually leave the company.'

Depression
'This really is happening and there is nothing I can do about it.'

Acceptance
'Well, this is how it is, but things aren't so bad.'

Moving on
'Actually this new set up is better than the old and I can see how I can make this work for me.'

TIME

(continued on next page)

ISBN: 9780170352598

What is a project champion?

A project champion is a person who has been identified to support and drive a project forward. This person can explain why it's happening, the benefits of the change, and may help the team and staff in dealing with the change so it becomes practice.

For example, if a business decided to adopt a new computer system, management might choose a well-respected and competent staff member to be fully trained in the new operating system to 'sell' the change to staff. The project champion may hear of issues before management and correct misconceptions before they become serious barriers to implementation.

Andrew will move staff through the cycle by having discussions as to how best to meet the new challenge of reduced deliveries, from denial and anger to the bargaining stage. Perhaps he could offer a better hourly rate to those part-time drivers, but this would increase costs. Or he could reallocate shifts to those who can work more at the shifts offered from those who can no longer work in the evenings. Staff may propose a better delivery method, such as batching deliveries and using better-insulated bags for the pizzas to keep them hot longer. If he adopts staff suggestions, and ensures staff understand the reality of the issues on the business, he may have moved the staff to acceptance and eventually moving on. For Heaven's Pizza, this may mean they have more efficient deliveries, lower costs overall, and improved customer satisfaction. Remaining staff may also appreciate that the change actually improved how they worked or the hourly rate, and how the communication built an element of trust and involvement beyond their initial role as driver, pizza maker or phone reception.

The operational issue I have chosen is _____		
Staff response	Change stage of model	Suggested business approach to move to next stage of model

　　ISBN: 9780170352598

case study 2

Downer set to pull out of Rangitikei as its depots close

Downer has confirmed it will close its depots in Marton and Taihape but it is not yet known how many jobs will be lost. The company employs 38 staff in the towns.

The closures follow this month's Rangitikei District Council decision to contract Manawatu-based company Higgins for roading work ahead of current contractors Downer. It was part of a joint agreement with Manawatu and Horowhenua District Councils.

'Absolutely, we are disappointed. But at the end of the day the council's made their decision,' Downer manager Chris Edsall said. The company had held the contract for 17 years.

There was no date for the depot closures but it would be after the council contract expired on 30 June.

Downer was talking to its Rangitikei employees about their future with the company.

'I'm going through that process at the moment. I can't really give you that info just yet,' Mr Edsall said.

He said staff were bitterly disappointed. 'Some of these staff have been there thirty years,' he said.

Staff had until today to give Downer feedback and Mr Edsall hoped to have a decision about their future with the company in the next week.

'We'll certainly be looking for other opportunities for our staff where possible. The reality is we won't be operating in Rangitikei in the future,' he said. 'We do do other work out of there, however it's not enough to sustain us.'

Downer's closest depots are in Wanganui and Palmerston North.

Councillors voted on the roading contract two weeks ago behind closed doors, due to commercial sensitivity. Earlier in that meeting, over 20 Marton business operators pleaded with council to retain Downer. They said changing the contractor would cost local jobs and hurt local business.

Rangitikei Mayor Andy Watson said it would save ratepayers about $1.3 million over three years.

You are a consultant contracted to help with the change management process for Downer staff. Using a model, work through the process identifying what staff, management and other stakeholders should be involved and in what ways. Focus on identifying the changes, what stakeholders are affected, and solutions to manage the change.

In your answer, build your answer in a structured manner, ensuring:

- TWO strategies to manage the changes are **explained**.
- The impacts of each strategy are **fully explained**. Provide a positive and negative impact of each strategy.
- A conclusion that justifies the better strategy.

(continued on next page)

A strategy is 'a plan of action or policy designed to achieve an overall aim'. In NCEA context, this means an action or policy that would apply to ALL parts of the business. An example would be for all products to be quality checked for dangerous chemicals prior to shipping to avoid consumer complaints.

What is a contingency plan?

A contingency plan is one that prepares an organisation's resources for unlikely events, including natural disasters, disruptions to supply chain, or IT failures. It is often referred to as the 'what if' plan.

tasks

1   The Board of Trustees has decided that all classes at the school will be streamed from next year, and reviewed every year based on end-of-year results across five subjects. This means students will be grouped in classes based on marks. The total marks of five subjects will determine if students are in the top or bottom class. You, as Principal, have to implement this change to staff and students. Brainstorm with your colleagues how this will happen. Apply a change management strategy to your school.

_____

_____

_____

2 Does your school have a uniform? If so, describe how you would implement a change to non-uniform from next year. Conversely, if you don't have a uniform either across the school or at a certain level such as Year 13, how would you implement a change to compulsory uniform for everyone?

_____

_____

_____

_____

_____

3 Research ONE of the following change management theorists. Now collaborate with other members of the class who have researched other models and share your knowledge. Create a bullet point guide to the five models for reference.

Definition of styles	
Kurt Lewin's Unfreeze-Change-Refreeze Model	
Stephen Covey's Seven Habits Model	
Kotter's 8-Step Change Model	
The ADKAR® Model	
Kubler-Ross Five-Stage Model	

ISBN: 9780170352598

4   a   Have a look at the following mergers that failed, and identify the change management process that might have helped the merger to be a success.

Definition of styles	
Daimler Benz – Chrysler	
Bank of America – Merrill Lynch	
AOL – Time Warner	

b   Then have a look at the following New Zealand mergers, and consider how the change management might have been handled. Identify the key factors that would have had to be considered by the parties involved.

Definition of styles	
Vodafone – Telstra Clear	
AMI – AIG	
Auckland City/ Waitakere City/ Manukau City and Rodney District – Auckland Council	

5   Explain how the merger of two businesses with different cultures can make success of the expansion less likely.

_____

_____

_____

_____

_____

6   Identify three recent changes in the external business environment that have had a dramatic impact on a New Zealand business.

i   _____

_____

_____

_____

_____

ii   _____

_____

_____

_____

_____

iii   _____

_____

_____

_____

_____

7   What role does planning have in change management? Explain with reference to a New Zealand business operating in a global context.

_____

_____

_____

_____

_____

_____

ISBN: 9780170352598

8 Identify from the following list of well-known New Zealanders what they are project champions for:

Alan Duff _____

Annah Stretton _____

Rob Fenwick _____

Pat Snedden _____

Lance O'Sullivan _____

Peter Gluckman _____

Guy Ryan _____

Stephen Tindall _____

Sam Judd _____

John Kirwan _____

Frances Valintine _____

9 NCEA-style question.

Zappos to employees:
Get behind 'no bosses' approach

Zappos.com CEO Tony Hsieh is offering an exit strategy to any workers who aren't sold on the unconventional idea.

No job titles. No traditional bosses. No conventional corporate hierarchy. It might sound nice, but would you really want to work there?

That's the question, essentially, that Zappos is asking its employees after experimenting with a radical approach to management. Called 'holacracy,' the new system replaces the conventional command-and-control workplace with a series of self-governed teams, known as 'circles.' The effort is supposed to speed decision-making, share authority and help the organisation become more innovative.

In a recent memo, Zappos CEO Tony Hsieh wrote that he is offering an exit strategy to any workers who aren't sold on the unconventional idea. If they are an employee in good standing and meet certain criteria, they can leave the online retailer and get at least three months' worth of severance.

In one sense, it's a way to help employees cope with radical change — while, in the process, filtering the employee pool of the least engaged folks. It's a fairly generous approach. When most companies roll out new strategies or new management tactics, after all, non-believers who voluntarily quit get little more than a handshake on their way out the door.

Hsieh's memo follows reports in the media that have critiqued the concept of 'holacracy' as impersonal, dogmatic and comically hard to explain. Others have cited complaints by Zappos employees who are frustrated with the new system.

ISBN: 9780170352598

John Bunch, who is helping to lead Zappos' transition to the new approach, said in an interview, 'There have been some people who've embraced those changes with open arms, and other people for whom maybe it [hasn't] resonated as strongly.' While he says the turnover hasn't been 'particularly high' yet due to the new approach, he would not share the company's forecasts for how many people it expects might accept the offer to leave.

So what will happen to the supervisors at Zappos who don't take the offer, given that the company plans to effectively eliminate traditional managers as of 30 April? Hsieh's memo says they will keep their salaries through to the end of 2015 and will get guidance for reinventing themselves into new roles at the company.

Bunch said he anticipates having no layoffs due to that change.

a Discuss the importance of effective leadership when dealing with employees' reaction to change. In your answer:

- fully explain, with examples, why it is important for a leader to be flexible with individuals when managing change
- fully explain an impact of the deadline proposed by Zappos on the performance of the business undergoing change.

ISBN: 9780170352598

b Evaluate TWO change management strategies for dealing with a change for Zappos. In your answer:

- explain TWO change management strategies that could be implemented when dealing with a management reporting change

- fully explain the impact of these strategies on the business by explaining ONE positive and ONE negative impact of EACH strategy on the performance of the business

- draw a justified conclusion as to which change management strategy would be more effective in this change situation.

_____

_____

_____

_____

_____

_____

_____

_____

_____

_____

_____

_____

_____

_____

_____

_____

_____

_____

 ISBN: 9780170352598

unit 2

Achievement Standard 90380 (3.2)

Demonstrate understanding of strategic response to external factors by a business that operates in a global context.

Students are expected to demonstrate understanding of the following business knowledge, concepts, and content:

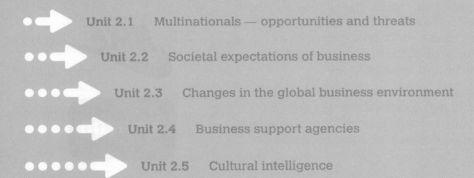

Unit 2.1   Multinationals — opportunities and threats

Unit 2.2   Societal expectations of business

Unit 2.3   Changes in the global business environment

Unit 2.4   Business support agencies

Unit 2.5   Cultural intelligence

ISBN: 9780170352598

Multinational Corporations (MNCs)

Historically, a business established in one country may have exploited resources in other countries to build wealth where a business is registered. For example, in the 19th century a British business may have sought relatively low value added gold ingot from New Zealand to be made into higher value goods in Britain and therefore greater wealth for the British shareholder. The greater integration of finance, trade and communications has resulted in the extension of the business model as globalisation becomes the norm.

Globalisation implies the opening of local and nationalistic perspectives to a broader outlook of an interconnected and interdependent world with free transfer of capital, goods and services across national frontiers. However, it does not include unhindered movement of labour and may hurt smaller or fragile economies if applied indiscriminately. Free trade is often the vital component in any move to *increase* globalisation. So how does an MNC fit?

A **multinational corporation** is an enterprise operating in several countries but managed from one (home) country. Generally, any company or group that derives a quarter of its revenue from operations outside of its home country is considered a multinational corporation.

tasks

1 From the above definition of an MNC, categorise the following as an MNC or not, and the main reason why/why not. The first one is done for you.

Enterprise	MNC: Yes/No?	Why/Why not?
Ford	Yes	Multiple production sites around world, e.g. USA, England, Brazil, with head office in Dearborn, Michigan, USA.
Sanitarium health & wellbeing		

BENDON		
BRISCOES HOMEWARE		
3M		
SAMSUNG		
the warehouse // where everyone gets a bargain		
Nestlé		
Fonterra		
Spark		
Heinz		
Pfizer		

2 a Research the following companies and determine their 'home' country.

Company	Home country	Company	Home country
Volvo		AXA Group	
Proctor and Gamble		BHP Billiton	
Tata		Bayer	
Caterpillar		Rio Tinto	
BP		L'Oreal	

   b Google 'who owns all the major brands' to see an image of the connections between companies. Go further and investigate who has what in media companies, especially the changes since 1890.

Why become an MNC?

Why does this globalisation and MNCs in particular matter? The most common reasons to become an MNC and move into other countries other than their home country are:

1 To be closer to the market. This can result in lower transport costs to finish, obtaining better information on the market, and the MNC may be looked at as a local company to build consumer loyalty. For example, McDonald's and the Kiwi burger plus the sponsorship of New Zealand junior soccer.

2 To obtain lower costs of production from any or all of the following:

   i lower labour costs compared with developed economies

   ii cheaper rent and site costs, which encourages location of production facilities and export opportunities

   iii central and local government incentives such as tax holidays or reduced company tax, government grants for establishment costs, and possibly fast-track regulatory procedures.

3 Access to local resources, including raw materials such as bauxite in Australia for aluminium production, oil in Saudi Arabia, or fish from the coast of New Zealand.

4 To avoid import restrictions. If you produce within a country, there will be no import duties and you may in fact have access to Government-paid export incentives.

So what are the issues around having multinational corporations operating in a host country?

tasks

3 After class discussions and some research, complete the following table with bullet points on each aspect with regard to the impact of the MNC operating in a country. Some have been done for you.

  ISBN: 9780170352598

Advantages	Disadvantages
Employment?	**Employment?**
Tax revenues to Government?	**Tax revenues to Government?**
GDP? Additional spending within the country on goods and services will increase GDP. Plus any exports will be higher value added, also improving GDP.	**Environment?**
For local firms?	**Competition?**
Investment?	**Cultural?**
Foreign exchange?	**Natural resources?**
Quality?	**Infrastructure?** The need to develop infrastructure (roads, ports) may stretch the financial resources of the country, diverting funds from health/education to MNC requirements.
Technology?	

ISBN: 9780170352598

4 a What is protectionism? Find a definition and explain why a country may adopt it as a policy? What is the opposite of protectionism?

b What policy does New Zealand adopt? What evidence do you have for its policy?

example

Discount giant Kmart has been secured as the new anchor tenant in the $15 million redevelopment of Bethlehem Town Centre. Centre manager Andrew Wadsworth, of Colliers International, has ended months of speculation by confirming the identity of the new tenant to the *Bay of Plenty Times Weekend*.

Mr Wadsworth said the team had been negotiating with Kmart for two years, and cited the arrival of the major retailer as another example of the significant growth the western Tauranga suburb was experiencing.

'This is a fantastic addition to the centre and the local community,' said Mr Wadsworth. 'A great deal of time and resource has gone into the planning of this project.'

Ben Smith, Kmart's Australia-based general manager of property, said he was pleased to bring Kmart to Bethlehem's residents and the greater Tauranga community.

'We're looking forward to developing our presence in Bethlehem,' said Mr Smith. 'At present our closest store is located in Mount Maunganui. There are currently 18 Kmart stores in New Zealand, and we're continually looking for new sites.

The new store will have 70–80 new staff made up of a combination of full-time, part-time and casual positions.

'The investment in the redevelopment by the centre's owners represents a significant measure of confidence in the centre and the region,' said Mr Wadsworth. 'And we have numerous conversations in the pipeline with various other retailers about coming to the centre.'

The redevelopment was expected to have between 30 and 50 tradespeople on site each day, increasing to 80 at peak times. Construction was due to begin next month, with Kmart due to open early next year.

 ISBN: 9780170352598

5   NCEA-style question.

a   Discuss the decision by Kmart to develop the Bethlehem outlet. In your answer:

   • explain the possible impact on other local retailers
   • fully explain a possible impact on future sales.

_____

_____

_____

_____

_____

_____

_____

_____

_____

_____

_____

_____

_____

b   A 'strategic response' means a business-wide reaction at multiple levels (size, scope and timeframe). Evaluate a possible strategic response by a New Zealand business such as The Warehouse, Briscoes, Farmers or a New Zealand-registered business of your choice to the plans by Kmart for the Tauranga market.

In your answer:

   • explain the chosen strategic response for the Tauranga market
   • fully explain ONE positive impact and ONE negative impact of the strategic response
   • draw a justified conclusion regarding the likely success of the strategic response to defend the local market of the business.

_____

_____

_____

_____

_____

_____

_____

_____

_____

_____

_____

_____

ISBN: 9780170352598

_____
_____
_____
_____
_____
_____

c   Having completed the above NCEA-style question for a
    local market such as Tauranga, now extend this to a new
    entrant into the New Zealand market such as Walmart
    (see www.news.walmart.com for more information) and
    take the position as CEO of any New Zealand-registered
    retail business.

    Again:

    •   explain the chosen strategic response for the New Zealand market
    •   fully explain ONE positive impact and ONE negative impact of the strategic response
    •   draw a justified conclusion regarding the likely success of the strategic response to defend the
        domestic market of the business.

_____
_____
_____
_____
_____
_____
_____
_____
_____
_____
_____
_____
_____
_____
_____
_____
_____
_____
_____
_____
_____

6 Further research

Investigate the arrival into New Zealand of David Jones, the high-end Australian retailer. In particular, the article below describes the 'attraction' effect of a retailer, and the impact on other businesses in the area both in terms of improving service and brand offering. Focus on a response by New Zealand business to such competition.

David Jones 'have to look at Auckland'

David Jones department store is planning to launch in Wellington next year with new brands and a complete building revamp for the old home of Kirkcaldie & Stains.

The retailer announced on Thursday that it was buying out the struggling Wellington institution Kirkcaldie & Stains for A$400,000 ($431,000) with an option to purchase its fixed assets for A$500,000 following a seven-year period of losses for the Wellington company.

David Jones chief executive Ian Nairn says the company is not planning on expanding beyond Wellington within the next few years but retail analysts say it is likely Auckland will see a David Jones store in the near future.

"The fact is while they'll be able to achieve some economies of scale, in terms of leveraging their [other brands for] logistics and warehousing and back office, having a store with the kind of population of the Wellington region is not really sustainable as one outpost," he says.

Following the announcement on Thursday, Nairn confirmed David Jones would spend more than $20 million on refurbishing the Wellington store before it opened midway through next year.

We will preserve the heritage-listed frontage whilst completely renovating the interior. Our aim is to create a world class shopping environment with the quality finishings and latest retail technology that shoppers expect from a premium department store says Ian Nairn.

New Zealand Retailers Association chief executive Mark Johnston says the smaller store size could prove difficult for the company.

"It will be a bit of a challenge but they'll have ideas and given Ian's background and also David Thomas the chief operating officer as well - both of them have come from Country Road and Witchery, also owned by Woolworth Holdings. So they know the New Zealand market quite well and have a good feel for it so they'll have ideas about what will work and what won't."

In Wilkinson's opinion the 152-year-old-Kirks has become stale in the retail sector and unlike some of the other department stores around New Zealand, is not at the heart of its community.

"The problem was when [Kirks] went through its remodelling in the 80s, it hasn't got the occasion that a department store typically has.

"Kirks doesn't have that and it misses some of the fundamentals in retail, like easy ways for consumers to get upstairs, and there's a whole lot of infrastructure issues that typify how the 80s was in terms of development. And in many ways those have been barriers for them to try and play in the market that they need to be playing in."

David Jones

- Leading Australian department store founded in 1838 in Sydney.
- Operates 35 stores and 2 warehouse outlets across Australia.
- Stocks over 1700 brands including its own David Jones line.
- The Wellington store is its first overseas outlet.

Consider the following strategic options for a New Zealand business (not in any order of preference):

1 Compete in service, quality or brand.
2 Merge with domestic competitor to build economies of scale to compete.
3 Discount product to hold market share.
4 Merge with incoming MNC.
5 Exit business/change product line.
6 Lobby Government for protection.
7 Reduce costs — staff, advertising, research and development, training, promotional activity, sponsorship, finance.

Discuss in groups the seven options. Fully explain ONE positive impact and ONE negative impact of each strategic response.

Draw a justified conclusion regarding the likely success of the strategic response to defend the domestic market of the business.

 ISBN: 9780170352598

2.2 Societal expectations of business

When we discuss the societal expectations of business we are looking at the interaction of the business on the wider fabric of society. This has been captured in an accounting framework and has evolved from economic reporting (financial performance of the business) to adding in environmental and social reporting to form the **Triple Line Reporting**. Sometimes this is quoted as the **'three Ps' — People, Planet and Profit**.

Quadruple bottom line reporting uses the idea of triple bottom line reporting as its foundation; it makes businesses accountable and responsible for the **economic, social, environmental and spiritual** effects of doing business. Although triple bottom line reporting (economic, environmental and social) is much more popular, the newer idea of quadruple bottom line reporting and the **addition of a spiritual aspect** is quickly gaining support. For our analysis, we will discuss spiritual in a **cultural aspect** — how the business operations might impact on the cultural aspects of the community.

Quadruple bottom line reporting requires an organisation to be responsible and accountable to **all** stakeholders of an organisation, not just the shareholders. **The stakeholders of an organisation are any people who are affected by the business activities of a company, including shareholders, customers, employees and suppliers**.

Any organisation using this form of accounting can increase business by positively building its reputation and public perception. The social aspect of quadruple bottom line reporting concentrates on the fair treatment of people by providing fair wages, a safe workplace and personal development opportunities.

Being socially responsible also requires performing responsible and beneficial business activities and practices within the community. A business using quadruple bottom line reporting must engage in sustainable environmental activities; the organisation should focus on reducing environmental harm through proper recycling, reducing waste, avoiding the production and use of harmful chemicals, and reducing energy consumption. The spiritual/cultural aspect of this form of reporting is concerned with discovering cultural fulfilment for all employees who dedicate their efforts and lives to the goals of the organisation.

Most people have difficulty determining the cultural aspect of a business, and society's expectations — so this will be looked at in depth.

Simply, how do the business operations impact positively or negatively on the cultural landscape?

For example, in New Zealand, does the business have rules or policies that act as barriers to some cultures (religious or ethnic), which would be a clear negative impact?

Or does the business have policies or operations that enhance cultures, such as consultation with Māori on land use or access to historical resources such as seafood?

example

THE WAREHOUSE GROUP

Our community partnerships have continued and strengthened over the past 12 months. We have maintained our focus on supporting organisations that work with families and young people with the goal of helping build a stronger and better New Zealand, now and in the future. Last year, more than 550 Kiwi organisations received funding from our community programmes at a national, regional and neighbourhood level. Once again, our community partners covered a wide spectrum, from local schools and community groups to organisations that supported families and young people across the country in the education, wellness and general social sectors.

The Warehouse continued to receive enormous support for our community partnerships from customers and suppliers and raised and distributed a total of $3,531,057.

We also continued to make progress on reducing landfill, increasing recycling, reducing our carbon footprint, and engaging and assisting our team and our customers to do the same. In addition, our dialogue with national and local government and our membership of organisations such as the Sustainable Business Council has enabled us to commence planning further activities, which will come to fruition over the coming years.

— *TWG Annual Report*

example

Hewlett Packard (HP)

HP has run a mentoring program for Year 13 students to help with career choices, business understanding and development of work skills. Schools involved have included Rangitoto College, Tamaki College, Avondale College, Otahuhu College and Aorere College. Hewlett-Packard staff volunteer their time to help the students because they want to, and the company provides time from work to do so if required. Students, staff and the company all benefit.

 ISBN: 9780170352598

tasks

1   Classify the activities of The Warehouse Group under the three headings in the table below — People, Planet and Profit. One example for Planet activities has been done for you.

People activities	Planet activities	Profit activities
	Reducing waste going to landfill by charging for plastic bags, which has seen plastic bag usage drop.	

2   Explain why The Warehouse Group incorporates these activities into its operations.

_____

_____

_____

_____

3   As The Warehouse Group grows in number of outlets, profit and employees, what would the societal expectations be on the organisation — more or less? Explain your answer.

_____

_____

_____

_____

_____

example

THE WAREHOUSE GROUP

'We are fully dedicated to ensuring our employment practices are free of any kind of discrimination based on gender, ethnic or national origins, colour, race, marital status, sexual orientation, age, disability, family status, employment status, religious belief, ethical belief, or political opinion.'

— TWG Diversity Policy August 2012

4 a Using the resource material from The Warehouse Group Diversity Policy document above, explain how this policy connects with societal expectations. Compare this policy with the legal requirements for non-discriminatory behaviour by an employer quoted at right.

_____

_____

_____

_____

_____

_____

_____

_____

_____

_____

_____

Discrimination

The law protects all people from unlawful discrimination; this includes discrimination on the grounds of:

* age
* race or colour
* ethnicity or national origins
* sex
* sexual orientation
* disability
* religious or ethical belief
* marital status
* employment status
* political opinion.

This means that an employer can't treat you differently (on the basis of your age or other grounds noted above) compared with other applicants or employees.

b Does The Warehouse Group policy go further than the law requires? Justify your answer and relate it to societal expectations.

_____

_____

_____

_____

_____

_____

_____

_____

_____

5   Using a business you have studied this year, review that organisation's activities under the Quadruple Bottom Line of Economic (sales, wages paid, tax paid, employment numbers, etc.), Environmental (minimising waste, recycling programmes, reuse of resources, reduction in CO_2 or pollutants/emissions, etc.), Social (activities with the community) and Cultural (activities to promote cultural aspects such as prayer rooms, consulting with iwi on impacts, multi-language signs in workplace, etc.).

Name of New Zealand registered business:

_____

2.3 Changes in the global business environment

The global business environment comprises a vast number of factors, most of which are beyond the control of a business. These factors could include government policies such as trade incentives; political unrest or uncertainty such as protests/demonstrations or simply the election cycle; changes in technology including information transfer and production methods; changes in consumer wants and desires; business competitors' strategies; exchange rate volatility; the labour market skills and mobility; and trade regulation.

While many of these factors are beyond the control of a single business, an awareness of the impact of any of the above is critical for the sustainability of a business wanting to operate in the global environment.

We will concentrate on the business needing to develop a strategic response to the following four key areas:

1 the impact of growth and recession on New Zealand export markets
2 political unrest
3 technology
4 consumer behaviour.

Key area 1: The impact of growth and recession on New Zealand export markets

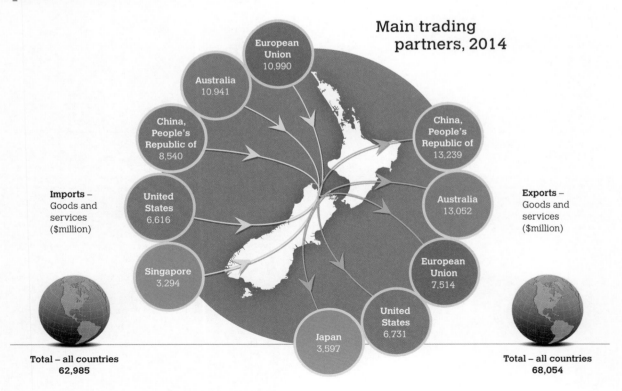

Main trading partners, 2014

European Union 10,990
Australia 10,941
China, People's Republic of 8,540
United States 6,616
Singapore 3,294

Imports – Goods and services ($million)

China, People's Republic of 13,239
Australia 13,052
European Union 7,514
United States 6,731
Japan 3,597

Exports – Goods and services ($million)

Total – all countries 62,985

Total – all countries 68,054

 ISBN: 9780170352598

New Zealand's export markets are literally everywhere. New Zealand exports to any country that is willing and able to buy New Zealand products, but the graphic on page 68 illustrates the top five markets we export to, are China, Australia, European Union, United States and Japan.

So what do we mean by the impact of growth and recession in these markets?

To start we need to define:

*   what is growth?
*   what is recession?

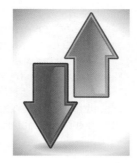

In economic terms, **growth** is measured by gross domestic product (GDP), which simply translates to the value of the goods and services produced within a country in a given time period (usually a year). It includes income from production carried out by New Zealanders and by foreign firms operating in New Zealand. We will let the economists argue over what should be in and shouldn't be in the calculation, so for our purposes we are focused on whether the country we are exporting to is growing and at what rate, or not growing as the case may be.

In economic terms, a **recession** is defined as two consecutive quarters (six months) of **negative** growth in GDP. This means the value of the goods and services produced in a country has declined in that six-month period.

So how does this affect a business looking to export its goods or services?

The table below summarises the impacts.

Export destination has economic growth	Export destination has a recession
An increase in the goods and services produced within a country will generally indicate more wealth for the residents of that country. As wealth increases through higher levels of employment, consumers will look to purchase greater quantities and higher quality goods and services that are often not available from domestic suppliers. Therefore there will be increased demand for imported goods and services, which means opportunities for New Zealand exporters.	As goods and services production declines in a country, this will generally mean a rise in unemployment as workers are no longer required and falling consumer incomes. The result is lower demand for goods and services whether imports or domestically produced. Exporters may therefore find the consumer market decreasing.
An increase in wealth usually means the government is increasing its revenue through taxes, fees and levies. Therefore many governments will encourage growth through trade with growing economies. For example by entering into trade agreements between countries that may make it easier for New Zealand exporters to enter another market.	The government facing a recession may concentrate its resources on reducing the impact on its unemployment levels by encouraging/subsidising domestic production. This can lead to trade barriers and the restriction of trade volumes, meaning a New Zealand exporter may become uncompetitive.

ISBN: 9780170352598

Increased government revenue will often translate into greater government expenditure on infrastructure to encourage continued economic growth. This infrastructure could include more efficient roading/rail/port facilities, which could translate to lower costs for the New Zealand exporter.	With less government revenues from taxation, governments may choose to encourage the purchase of locally produced goods through a 'Buy NZ' campaign, which may encourage domestic producers to increase production and in turn begin exporting themselves. The New Zealand exporter may therefore find themselves blocked from a market and also facing another international competitor.
With New Zealand only approximately 4.5 million people, the opportunity to reach a larger market and obtain economies of scale in production/finance/marketing or supply chain may be attractive to a New Zealand exporter.	A country suffering from recession can result in the movement of people out of the country to other countries with the prospects of greater wealth and higher standard of living. The movement of consumers from one country to another may mean the New Zealand producer/exporter loses domestic market share unless they trade with the country where those consumers have gone.
Economic growth in a trading partner (e.g. Australia) may see the exchange rate between the two countries change. This may mean an exporting country such as New Zealand may have a benefit in a lower exchange rate relative to the country exporting to. This simply means that exports will be seen as a cheaper purchase than domestic supplies or goods/services from other countries.	A country suffering from recession may see the value of its currency fall relative to New Zealand's. This means New Zealand exporters will get less revenue for its exports and the goods/services will be relatively more expensive in the overseas market. This simply means the New Zealand exporter may find this export market no longer viable.

The table below shows how GDP can be affected — and why the New Zealand Government encourages investment and exporters. Both are valuable contributors to growing New Zealand GDP, which in turn is taken as a measure of increasing the standard of living of consumers within that country.

Size of the economy (GDP)		$240 billion
Increases GDP	Household spending	$135 billion
	Government	$45 billion
	Investment	$55 billion
	Exports	$65 billion
Decreases GDP	Imports	$65 billion

18 June 2015, Department of Statistics

tasks

1 In your own words, summarise why a New Zealand exporter needs to consider the economic performance of a trading partner.

_____

_____

_____

_____

_____

_____

_____

_____

2 Research the trend in migration, GDP performance, exchange rate and export volumes of Australia and New Zealand over the past five years. Use the Department of Statistics website or any other relevant website. What conclusions can you make?

_____

_____

_____

_____

_____

_____

_____

_____

3 While the infographic on page 68 shows the key markets New Zealand trades with, what are the main product groups? Research the Department of Statistics to find the top five exports for New Zealand. At the same time, what were the top five products in 1990 and 1960? What important changes have taken place in regard to products and markets? Suggest two reasons why this has happened.

_____

_____

_____

_____

_____

_____

_____

ISBN: 9780170352598

4   From the data gathered in Task **3**, what strategies do you think New Zealand exporters learnt in regard to overseas markets and products?

_____

_____

_____

_____

_____

_____

_____

_____

_____

The Business Cycle

One last area in regard to exporters into any market is the Business Cycle, and how a business needs to evaluate its strategy against the changing cycle. This means being aware of when the economy is expanding (growth) and contracting (recession), and having plans in place to mitigate any negative impacts but also take advantage of any positive influences such as increased incomes for consumers. For an exporter, there are also considerations such as inflation, investment availability, interest rates and employment levels to consider as the country moves through the cycle.

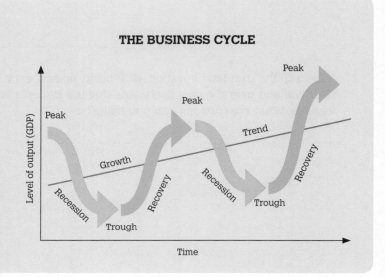

THE BUSINESS CYCLE

tasks

5   Refer to the Business Cycle above. Inflation is likely to appear at the peak of the cycle — why? And what will employment levels be like at the recession/trough part of the cycle?

_____

_____

_____

_____

_____

_____

Fonterra bosses face hard decisions

Read the headlines and you could be forgiven for thinking the country is being pushed into a major recession through slumping dairy prices.

It is a long way from when New Zealand commanded the reputation as the 'Saudi Arabia of milk' and Fonterra chiefs boasted when revealing their financial results of how many billions the dairy export trade was bringing into the NZ economy.

These days the mood is resigned. But farmers are resilient and focused on the medium and longer-term future.

The long slump in dairy prices combined with concerns the Chinese domestic consumer market is coming off the boil is causing a rethink in banking quarters.

But what really counts are the strategic decisions around the Fonterra board table in the coming weeks.

Fonterra chief executive Theo Spierings has been in Europe extending the co-operative's global footprint with the opening of a plant in the Netherlands.

It is a big move for Fonterra: the first time it has opened a wholly owned and operated ingredients plant in Europe, processing one billion litres of milk each year, and producing 5000 metric tonnes of whey protein and 25,000 metric tonnes of lactose annually.

It's clearly part of the international strategy that Spierings has spearheaded. He has pointed to Fonterra's substantial intellectual property in manufacturing functional whey protein ingredients as a key driver in the new partnership: 'Having a high-quality, high-volume source based in Europe will allow us to commercialise these innovations for our customers all over the world.'

Fonterra says it will increase its chances in a globally traded whey protein and lactose market that is worth more than $2.7 billion in 2014.

Spierings would have welcomed the opportunity to get offshore and expand Fonterra's business at a time when the domestic focus has been on the downside.

The company restructuring that Fonterra embarked on before the top brass left for Europe is working through.

Word is that the restructuring is likely to involve considerably more casualties than the hundreds that Spierings inadvertently hinted at in a radio interview.

From a farmer perspective, what matters is whether the co-operative will also lower its existing payout forecast of $5.25 kg/milk solids for the coming year.

If that occurs the Reserve Bank can be expected to move further with its accommodative interest rates easing policy.

One plus is that an exporter-friendly Kiwi dollar is helping soften the impact of poor dairy prices.

But the impact of the price trough has been exacerbated by the fact that the current dairy prices are below the cost of production.

Economists expect the impact of low prices to kick in, leading to a slowdown in production growth next year.

Cameron Bagrie, chief economist at ANZ (NZ) sends a warning that lower dairy prices will knock more off our terms of trade than the Reserve Bank has been projecting.

Bagrie says that will be a bigger economic hit and means there is more work for monetary policy to do to stabilise the economy.

What he hasn't done is mention the R word.

6 Using the resource material on Fonterra, and after conducting some of your own research, complete the following questions.

a What impact will the lower payout to dairy farmers have on the New Zealand economy?

_____

_____

_____

_____

ISBN: 9780170352598

b   Why will the Reserve Bank adjust interest rates?

_____

_____

_____

_____

c   What will be the effect on investment into New Zealand, and by businesses in New Zealand?

_____

_____

_____

_____

d   Why will low prices result in lower production?

_____

_____

_____

_____

e   Why has Fonterra built overseas processing plants? What is the strategy? Where else is Fonterra building?

_____

_____

_____

_____

_____

_____

f   Is there any connection to the Business Cycle in the resource material?

_____

_____

_____

_____

g   What is monetary policy? Define and give an example for New Zealand.

_____

_____

_____

_____

Key area 2: Political unrest

Unrest no bar to expansion into Egypt

BurgerFuel does not expect political events to affect entry into Cairo market

Burgerfuel's store in Saudi Arabia.

BurgerFuel isn't letting Egypt's violent political unrest — which has resulted in close to 100 deaths — stand in the way of its latest international expansion plans.

The NZX-listed fast food operator has begun construction on two stores in the Egyptian capital, Cairo, which has seen widespread bloodshed since anti-government demonstrations began on 30 June. BurgerFuel chief executive Josef Roberts said the company did not expect the events to have any impact on its entry into the Egyptian market and the Cairo stores were expected to open within the next few months.

'While there is great unrest, life goes on,' he said. 'As a franchisor, our local franchisee is the one who is operating the stores and if they're happy with the conditions then we are generally guided by them.'

The Auckland-based firm's Egyptian franchisee, Wadi Degla, has business interests across a number of sectors including telecommunications, property development and food and beverage.

BurgerFuel, which opened a store in Iraq last year, had benefited from making its push into the Middle East during a volatile period in the region's history, he added.

Roberts said people often wondered how the company had managed to secure such good retail sites in Dubai.

'We went in there during the GFC [Global Financial Crisis] so we were able to negotiate real estate and able to negotiate leases,' he said. 'There is a positive side to going into these countries when they're not in a good state.'

BurgerFuel reported total store system sales — which includes franchisees' revenue — of $49.3 million for the 12 months to 31 March, an increase of 29.2 per cent on the previous year.

The franchisor's profit came in at $1 million, up from $708,360 a year earlier. BurgerFuel shares, which have gained 71 per cent over the past 12 months, closed steady at $1.80 last night.

BurgerFuel's current store count:

- 30 — New Zealand
- 1 — Australia
- 7 — United Arab Emirates
- 5 — Saudi Arabia
- 1 — Iraq
- 44 — Total

task

7 a What possible issues would BurgerFuel NZ have in establishing the stores in Egypt, Iraq and the next possible store, Libya? Consider safety of employees, stability of financial system, supply of ingredients, infrastructure supply including water/gas/electricity and waste removal, security of assets, communications, access to the country.

_____

_____

_____

---

b What is the New Zealand Government's expectation for New Zealand business people in areas of political unrest? Research the Ministry of Foreign Affairs website at www.safetravel.govt.nz to see current travel advisories.

ISBN: 9780170352598

Key area 3: Technology

Technology continues to advance at a rapidly increasing rate, with new products available that would never have been dreamed about 20 years ago such as wi-fi internet, Facebook, electric cars, Cookies and Cream ice cream, and access to new channels to markets.

The impact of technology has been substantial in accessing the global marketplace.

- Distances have 'decreased', making the world a global marketplace as communication between members of the supply chain becomes easier, especially through social media such as Twitter, Facebook, etc.

- Accessibility to products has increased through the click of a mouse.

- What was once a niche market in a country can now be a substantial global market that will enable economies of scale.

- The rise of Big Data — a collection of data from traditional and digital sources inside and outside a business that represents a source for ongoing discovery and analysis.

- Transactions can be global. Do you really know *where* you are buying a product from if it's bought from Amazon?

For a business, it is a matter of survival to stay up-to-date with technological advances. Consider a retailer without a website or not being able to sell online, or operating without email.

Possible advantages of technological change	Possible disadvantages of technological change
If you're first to market with a new product, you will lead the market and have a competitive advantage in a global marketplace, e.g. Toyota Prius or Coca-Cola.	Costs of developing or maintaining technological systems can be expensive, therefore a business may not be able to afford new systems and become less competitive over time.
New technology in production equipment may boost productivity and therefore lower average costs, making the business more competitive.	A business that does not develop new products or services will eventually lose sales to global competitors and go out of business.
Business can use the internet for direct sales to consumers without incurring 'bricks and mortar' costs of retail stores, reducing costs and possibly increasing sales.	The need to maintain data protection — for customer records and business records as well. The threat of viruses and the illegal use of data is a major concern and cost for business.

ISBN: 9780170352598

New technology in equipment may require fewer workers to manage, and therefore also fewer management staff required. Reduced costs.	The costs of frequent market research and regularly developing new products may be beyond some companies' finances, especially small businesses. Large-scale global businesses may now be a local producer's biggest competitor.
New production equipment often enables a business to become more flexible in production of goods and services, such as smaller production runs and variation on product design, e.g. iPhone now in various colours.	As the reliance on computer systems increases, so will the costs of a failure of the system impact. For example, the loss of internet for an online retailer.
Technology has enabled businesses to consider the international market for sales, with improved delivery systems and online payment, e.g. Xero, Amazon, Pumpkin Patch.	Collection of Big Data may be beyond small businesses, making them uncompetitive.
Social media such as Twitter, Facebook and Instagram can be a major communication channel for talking directly to customers. Smartphones are predicted to grow significantly as devices for shopping, with new payment methods (Apple Pay, payWave, etc.).	Social media can be misleading. What was an 'urban myth' in a domestic market can now be a global story that may destroy a company's reputation, whether true or false.
Big Data — the accumulation and analysis of people across the globe will drive personalised marketing programmes. Consumers will be made aware of products tailored to them without needing to look.	Internet fraud, as criminals use software to capture payment data, including identity theft.

tasks

8   Find out about Big Data, and its impact on market research. What value will this data have on a business looking to participate in the global marketplace?

_____

_____

_____

_____

_____

_____

_____

_____

_____

Hitching NZ up to disruptive tech's cart

Kiwis have started disruptive businesses ranging from local beauty salon booking apps to rockets aimed at flying satellites to space but more could be thinking bigger, say sector leaders.

A survey of chief executives by PwC showed the proportion of them worried about the speed of technological change had risen from 37 per cent in 2014 to 68 per cent this year.

Economic Development Minister Steven Joyce said his government did not want to get in the way of innovation by adding complexity. It was, however, supporting companies through the Callahan Institute with potential through matched funding and tax incentives.

The Government wanted to be reasonably neutral about technology and industry it followed rather than 'second guess' it. One indicator of the disrupters' success — exports of software — was showing strong growth, said Joyce.

New Zealand's distance from the rest of the world had traditionally been a barrier for physical exports but technology meant smart firms here could easily operate overseas.

'The flip side of international competition is an international marketplace,' he said.

New Zealand risks missing out on fully capitalising on disruptive technology and business models, says Greg Doone, PwC's digital strategy and data leader.

Traditional retail and entertainment content businesses were on what Doone said was an endangered list rather than doomed.

The competitive threat was changing and it will not necessarily be local or vertical.

'Will the disruption to the supermarkets come from each other or elsewhere?' In the United States the main threat to supermarkets was Amazon through which customers now ordered their groceries.

New Zealand retailers were being hurt by online shopping overseas. The percentage of retail goods bought online from overseas sites had grown from 28 per cent in 2013 to 42 per cent in the past year.

'You don't necessarily have big financial alerts above New Zealand retailers, however there's a massive market share they've missed out on.'

'We think we need to export more and take some of the load away from the primary sector — they've done a fantastic job of being export focused and the rest of us need to move away from just providing domestic services and build export businesses' Doone said.

9 What are 'disrupters'? Hint: three are Uber, Airbnb, Netflix.

_____

_____

_____

10 'The flip side of international competition is an international marketplace.' Evaluate this statement with reference to a New Zealand-registered business.

_____

_____

11 Visit your local supermarket, especially the fruit and vegetable area. Where are these products coming from, and how are New Zealand consumers now in the 'global marketplace'?

Big Data mining – how the numbers can affect you

- Prisoners in Pennsylvania face having the chance of their reoffending impacting on the amount of time they spend in jail under a new plan. Those less likely to reoffend will be released sooner, while those judged to be a risk face a longer sentence.

- In the US, credit card customers have had their credit limits cut after a data analysis of shopping patterns showed they had shopped at the same stores as people with poor credit histories. Statistically, it made them a greater risk.

- Car registration differ depending on the likelihood of accidents happening to people driving a particular type of car. The idea of the Big Data crunch was to reward those who pose the least risk.

12 Use the resource on Big Data mining to answer the following.

a Would you consider that prisoners in Pennsylvania are being treated fairly as outlined?

b What impact would the cut in credit limits have on the retailers, credit card companies and consumers?

c The car registration costs have changed for New Zealand in 2015. Can you think of any issues that the data used to calculate the registrations caused?

 ISBN: 9780170352598

Key area 4: Consumer behaviour

What is consumer behaviour? It is the process by which individuals search for, review, choose, buy, consume and dispose of goods and services, in satisfaction of their needs and wants. In other words, how and what we buy as consumers.

The main catalyst that triggers the buying decision of an individual is the need for a particular product/service. **Consumers purchase products and services as and when the need arises.**

People are bombarded with messages trying to influence their consumer behaviour. While we are familiar with the role of marketing and advertising, what about the more subtle aspects of measuring and influencing behaviour to assist us to believe we have a 'need', such as:

- product placement in movies, online ads, etc.
- push advertising — visiting a website that records your interest and supplies that information to similar products to follow you as you move from website to website. Do you think it was a coincidence that the same ad shows up on three different websites?
- social media — after all, when you 'like' something, what happens to that message among your friends or online connections?

When need arises, consumers search for information that would help them in the purchase. The main sources of information are:

- personal sources, e.g. friends, family
- commercial sources, e.g. trade magazines, consultants, business associations
- public sources, e.g. online forums, web reviews
- personal experience, e.g. actual purchase experiences driving confidence in a brand such as HP.

Buying decisions of consumers also depend on the following factors:

- Messages, advertisements and promotional materials that consumers go through, also called **selective exposure**.
- Not all promotional materials and advertisements excite consumers. Consumers do not pay attention to everything they see. They are interested in only what they want to see. Such behaviour is called **selective attention**.
- **Consumer interpretation** is how an individual perceives a particular message.
- Consumers would certainly buy something that appeals to them the most. They would remember the most relevant and meaningful message, called **selective retention**. They would obviously not remember something that has nothing to do with this need.

tasks

13 Complete the table below with examples from your knowledge and discussion with others. In some cases, the examples will operate in more than one area. For example, Facebook is a personal service, but is now used commercially to get messages to consumers, and has a sharing aspect ('Likes'), which means personal experience can be shared with other consumers. When you have a great experience, what do people now do?

Personal sources	Commercial sources	Public sources	Personal experience

14 Consider the New Zealand-registered business that you have studied, or plan to study in depth for the exam. How does it interact with consumers, and influence consumer behaviour?

_____

_____

_____

_____

_____

15 a Use the resource on page 83 and explain how consumer behaviour is being or not being valued, and assess the likely impact on the business.

_____

_____

_____

_____

_____

_____

_____

Outrage over Milo recipe change

A new recipe for the Milo chocolate drink is not going down well with some customers..

A change to Milo's recipe has caused outrage among fans of the chocolatey drink, who say it now tastes 'gross and disgusting'.

A Facebook page, 'Change Milo back to the old recipe', is pleading for a change of heart from makers Nestlé.

The page has 501 likes, with many disgruntled consumers saying they won't buy Milo any more.

Mum Taryn Ibell, who started the Facebook page, said she discovered the change after opening a new packet last week. 'It tasted disgusting. Like all malt and nothing else.'

Many others also commented that their families weren't happy with the new taste.

Rachel Lee wrote: 'With three teenage boys in the house we go through A LOT of Milo each week. My boys are not happy and I agree, the new recipe tastes awful! If it doesn't get changed back, I won't be buying it again!'

On the Milo Australia and New Zealand Facebook page, the company was also fielding angry complaints about the change.

In response to one complaint, the company said: 'We've made a small change to our New Zealand recipe in order to focus on the four primary ingredients that make up MILO, which are milk powder, malt barley, sugar and cocoa.'

In response to another complaint, it explained: 'We've just recently adjusted the vitamins and minerals in MILO so now it is delivering a balance of vitamins to really support energy production to help active kids, and adults, perform at their best. We've added vitamins D, B3, B6 and B12 and taken out vitamins A and B1 and magnesium.'

Nestlé spokeswoman Margaret Stuart said there were no plans to change the formula despite the protest.

While she admitted there had been a slight shift in flavour, the drink's four main components remained the same. The changes were part of a global change to Milo, Ms Stuart said.

'[The changes] reflect our research into the nutritional needs of children.'

---

b   What research would it appear Nestlé *did not* do for New Zealand consumers?

_____

_____

_____

_____

_____

c   How have consumers expressed their preference for this product change? What sources of information are being used?

_____

_____

_____

_____

_____

d   Why do you think Nestlé made this change? Evaluate the outcome for Nestlé; use the term 'consumer behaviour' in your answer.

_____

_____

_____

_____

_____

e   Will this change affect only New Zealand consumers? What is the impact on consumers globally, if any?

_____

_____

_____

_____

f   What other products from any other manufacturer have experienced changes that have or have not met with consumer acceptance?

_____

_____

_____

_____

_____

_____

_____

_____

_____

_____

_____

_____

   ISBN: 9780170352598

Business support agencies

There are a number of agencies that aim to support business in a number of ways. We shall look at governmental agencies such as New Zealand Trade and Enterprise (NZTE), Companies Office and Immigration New Zealand, and non-governmental agencies such as BusinessNZ and New Zealand Manufacturers and Exporters Association. Many local councils also have support agencies, including Auckland Tourism, Events and Economic Development (ATEED), Wellington Regional Economic Development Agency (WREDA) and Canterbury Development Corporation (CDC).

Governmental agencies

NZTE is the Government's international business development agency. Its purpose is to grow companies internationally for the benefit of New Zealand.

How? By increasing New Zealand companies' international success by helping them connect with markets and build capability to supply market requirements. NZTE currently works with around 4000 New Zealand businesses, and focuses intensively on around 700 of these customers. Visit the website for extensive information about how it assists New Zealand exporters and investors into New Zealand.

ISBN: 9780170352598

Services offered by NZTE to New Zealand exporters

NZTE has a great section on its main website describing its International Marketing and Communication Toolkit, with links to key areas for any business exporting from New Zealand.

Visit the section labelled 'How NZTE can help' and progress to 'Getting help to grow internationally' to see the wide range of support programmes the organisation provides illustrated by the web shot below.

ISBN: 9780170352598

Map of available resources through NZTE offices

The map on the right shows the locations of the 38 NZTE offices worldwide. The larger the dot the more resources are available (e.g. Los Angeles, Sao Paulo, London, Dubai). In this context, 'resources' refers to people and their expertise, along with actual physical workspaces so New Zealand exporters can book meeting rooms. to meet with potential customers in a hope to secure business. Full details on locations and resources can be seen on the NZTE website.

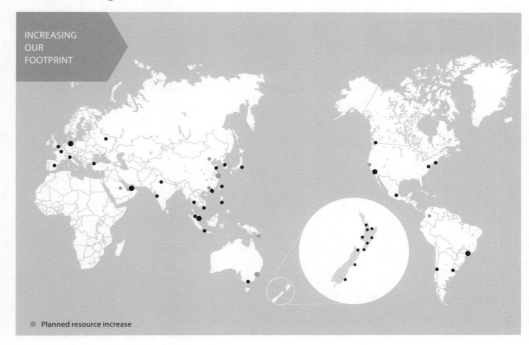

INCREASING OUR FOOTPRINT

● Planned resource increase

task

1   Why is there no representation in Africa, Norway/Sweden, Russia? Suggest two reasons.

_____

_____

_____

_____

_____

Business portal for New Zealand companies

The Companies Office via www.Business.govt.nz has practical online information and resources specifically designed for helping small and medium-sized businesses.

Immigration New Zealand (INZ) is part of the Ministry of Business, Innovation and Employment.
INZ is responsible for bringing suitable people to New Zealand to build New Zealand's social and economic outcomes. They support New Zealand's labour market by attracting people to New Zealand and helping them into the workforce so they become long-term contributors. INZ also contributes to key export industries such as tourism and education (e.g. such as international students).

The role of INZ in supporting New Zealand business includes:

* deciding visa applications
* attracting appropriate migrant skills and labour
* matching migrant skills with New Zealand employer needs.

tasks

2   From one of the agencies' websites, determine a strategy it uses to support New Zealand business to grow internationally.

_____

_____

_____

_____

_____

_____

_____

_____

3   What type of threats could a New Zealand exporter face in building its business overseas?

_____

_____

_____

_____

_____

_____

_____

_____

_____

Individualism versus collectivism — does it matter?

A business operating overseas will often come up against a different attitude to how/why people or businesses participate in society. One way is to classify the society as individualist, which is a social theory favouring freedom of action for individuals *over* collective or state control. Another is to classify a society as collective, where a group has priority *over* each individual in it. For example, when the ownership of land and the means of production is by the people or the state.

Here are two examples:

1   'Encouragement has been given to individualism, free enterprise, and the pursuit of profit.'
2   'The Russian Revolution decided to alter the course of modernity towards collectivism.'

task

4   Considering the two examples on page 88, what country can be generalised as being example 1, and which might be example 2?

_____

_____

Answer: USA for 1, and currently China and to some extent Fiji (land ownership) and New Zealand for 2.

Ten differences between collectivist and individualist societies

Individualism	Collectivism
Everyone is supposed to take care of him- or herself and his or her immediate family only	People are born into extended families or clans which protect them in exchange for loyalty
'I' – consciousness	'We' – consciousness
Right of privacy	Stress on belonging
Speaking one's mind is healthy	Harmony should always be maintained
Others classified as individuals	Others classified as in-group or out-group
Personal opinion expected: one person, one vote	Opinions and votes predetermined by in-group
Transgression of norms leads to guilt feelings	Transgression of norms leads to shame feelings
Languages in which the word 'I' is indispensable	Languages in which the word 'I' is avoided
Purpose of education is learning how to learn	Purpose of education is learning how to do
Task prevails over relationship	Relationship prevails over task

What does this mean for business?

Within New Zealand, collectivism is often seen in Māori activities, where the 'we' is often more important than the individual, for example in the use of resources such as land or harvesting seafood. Overseas, this can also be important, such as land ownership in Fiji or China.

A business setting up in a collective society therefore needs to be aware of the 'we' in terms of employing people (families and relatives will be favoured on recruitment), how decisions are made (vote rather than one decision-maker) and the objectives as they relate to the society (profit or long-term social improvement).

A simple comparison can be in employing someone in an individualistic society — profit or financial benefit will drive behaviour so a commission system will work well. In the collective, a team approach to a task will bring more benefits than an individual reward, such as the provision of health care to a community or computers to a school.

ISBN: 9780170352598

task

5 a In New Zealand, how would you classify most businesses — collective or individualistic? Why?

_____

_____

_____

_____

b Whale Watch Kaikoura is a good example of a collective approach to business. Research its website and identify why it operates — is it for the benefit of the owners or for the community?

_____

_____

_____

_____

_____

_____

c Can a business be both collective and individualistic? Explain your view with an example.

_____

_____

_____

_____

_____

The New Zealand Trade and Enterprise website (www.nzte.govt.nz) has an excellent section on cultural differences to be aware of. For example, on the China section of the website, it goes into depth explaining how to build trust, how not to offend, and how to negotiate. For example:

Numbers and colours to avoid

There are traditional taboos around numbers. Some business people are especially sensitive to numbers in China, especially in the southern part of China.

Lucky numbers:

3 When pronounced in Chinese, especially Cantonese (spoken in Guandong province and Hong Kong), sounds similar to the word for promotion or being promoted	**6** When pronounced in Cantonese is similar to the word for happiness	**8** When pronounced in Chinese sounds like a similar word that means prosperity	**168** When pronounced in Chinese sounds like a similar phrase that means money flowing in easily

Unlucky numbers to be avoided:

4 When pronounced in Chinese, sounds like the word for death (especially in Guangdong province and Hong Kong)

250 When pronounced in Chinese, sounds like the word for dumb/stupid

In some lifts, you'll find there is no number for the 4th, 13th or 14th floors.

Red and gold are for happy occasions. Black and white are for funerals.

task

6 a How would a New Zealand business manage the numbers on page 90 and above in negotiating prices?

_____

_____

_____

_____

b If a New Zealand business used black and white in its logo, what issues might they face in the Chinese market? What possible solutions might you suggest to reduce or avoid those issues?

_____

_____

_____

_____

c Discuss among your class what protocols might be expected to be observed in countries other students or staff have visited. For example, when entering a room for a meeting with Japanese businessmen, where do you (as CEO) sit and where does the most junior staff member of your business sit? The answer is: you sit directly opposite the highest ranked person from the other business as a sign of respect. Your junior staff likewise sits opposite someone of similar ranking. It is an insult to have a junior staff member sitting opposite a CEO!

_____

_____

_____

_____

ISBN: 9780170352598

Non-governmental agencies

These agencies are often partly funded by councils or through memberships by trade organisations, and will provide advice and connections to develop business expansion.

- Specialist business advisers (usually from local economic development agencies or Chambers of Commerce) who provide advice, information, referrals and connections. For example, Auckland Chamber of Commerce.
- Te Puni Kokiri: Advice and guidance to new and existing Māori businesses through the Māori Business Facilitation Service.
- BusinessNZ: Business advocacy group offering online guides and tools, reports and publications. Its aim is sustainable growth through free enterprise.
- Business Mentors New Zealand: Experienced business mentors share their knowledge and expertise with businesses to help them grow.
- Employers and Manufacturers Association (EMA): Business advice, education and training.

tasks

7   Research one of the non-governmental agencies above and explain what assistance they could provide to a New Zealand-registered business looking to expand globally. Why would a local business use these agencies?

_____

_____

_____

_____

_____

_____

_____

_____

8   BusinessNZ refers to 'free enterprise'. What is this? Compare it to the New Zealand political system. Is there any connection between business and politics? Explain your answer.

_____

_____

_____

_____

_____

_____

_____

_____

_____

2.5 Cultural intelligence

What is cultural intelligence? It is defined as someone's ability to adapt successfully to a new cultural setting. In business, it's the ability of the business to adapt to new markets, to have an appreciation of the cultural mix of its customers and workforce, and to build a sustainable business across cultures.

Cultural intelligence is related to emotional intelligence, but it goes a step further. People with high *emotional* intelligence can pick up on the emotions, wants and needs of others. Those with high *cultural* intelligence are attuned to the values, beliefs and attitudes of people from different cultures; and they use this knowledge to interact with empathy and understanding. In a business context, cultural intelligence is the ability of the organisation to use observation, empathy and intelligence to read people and situations, and to make informed decisions about why people act as they do, and adjust their own actions accordingly.

For example, these brand campaigns were unsuccessful:

Clairol launched a curling iron called 'Mist Stick' in Germany even though '*Mist*' is German slang for manure.

Coca-Cola's brand name, when first marketed in China, was sometimes translated as 'Bite the Wax Tadpole.'

Colgate launched toothpaste in France named 'Cue' without realising that it's also the name of a French pornographic magazine.

Coors translated its slogan, 'Turn It Loose', into Spanish, where it is a colloquial term for having diarrhoea.

 Ford blundered when marketing the Pinto in Brazil because the term in Brazilian Portuguese means 'tiny male genitals'.

Gerber marketed baby food in Africa with a cute baby on the label without knowing that, in Ethiopia, for example, products usually have pictures on the label of what's inside since many consumers can't read.

KFC made Chinese consumers a bit apprehensive when 'finger-licking good' was translated as 'eat your fingers off'.

Electrolux at one time marketed its vacuum cleaners in the US with the tag line: 'Nothing sucks like an Electrolux.'

Mercedes-Benz entered the Chinese market under the brand name 'Bensi', which means 'rush to die'.

 Nike had to recall thousands of products when a decoration intended to resemble fire on the back of the shoes resembled the Arabic word for Allah.

Parker Pen, when expanding into Mexico, mistranslated 'It won't leak in your pocket and embarrass you' into 'It won't leak in your pocket and make you pregnant.'

 Pepsi's slogan 'Pepsi Brings You Back to Life' was debuted in China as 'Pepsi Brings You Back from the Grave'.

tasks

1 Fully explain how cultural intelligence of export markets will support a New Zealand-registered business in achieving its strategic plan of expanding internationally. In your answer:

a explain the importance of cultural responsiveness and intelligence in the global marketplace

_____

_____

_____

_____

_____

b fully explain the impact on sales of their products if the company's strategy lacks cultural responsiveness and intelligence.

_____

_____

_____

_____

_____

_____

_____

_____

Agribusiness: Approach success by design

Matthijs Siljee, a professor at Massey University's College of Creative Arts.

Understanding other cultures is key to New Zealand making its food attractive to different markets around the world and to boosting our export earnings, according to a top industrial designer.

Matthijs Siljee, a Dutch professor at Massey University's College of Creative Arts, believes selling more of the same thing won't achieve the Government's goal of tripling the value of food exports by 2025. 'Anyone can see it is madness to try to pump out even more milk powder. That is not where the value is going to come from.'

Instead he says the country needs to take a design-led approach to developing new food products.

But Siljee says it's not always easy to nail down what appeals to certain consumers — especially when it comes to other countries. 'You cannot make assumptions ... You have to know the culture inside out to know what is wrong or right for a brand.'

Siljee says when it comes to food, one recent success is Zespri's special yellow spoon, which it sells packaged with its gold kiwifruit into international markets.

 ISBN: 9780170352598

'People buy the fruit and keep the spoon and it provides a semi-reminder. It is designed specially for that fruit and is part of the branding strategy. That is an example of how design works.'

Massey is undertaking design work through Open Lab, part of its College of Creative Arts. One of the areas it is working on is a knife to go with butternut squash sold into the Korean and Asian markets in their off season. Butternut is difficult to cut safely and that is one of the main things that turns consumers off, so work has begun on designing a knife to be sold alongside.

Siljee says the best way to learn about a market is to connect with the people who live there. 'We need to immerse ourselves with people from those markets.'

That's a big challenge when it comes to a place like China, which has so many regional language and cultural difference. Siljee says there are no short-cuts. 'Nothing is cheap. We have to be a world leader in understanding cultures.'

2 a Using the resource material above and your own knowledge, what lessons do New Zealand businesses need to consider when developing products or services to foreign markets?

_____

_____

_____

_____

b With reference to a New Zealand-registered business you have studied, identify what cultural intelligence the business will need to gather to ensure the move to expand is successful.

_____

_____

_____

_____

c Why are live sheep exports not acceptable to some New Zealanders, yet acceptable to Saudi Arabia? What alternative supply of sheep meat to Saudi Arabia has cultural protocols?

_____

_____

_____

_____

3 Choose one of the following popular export markets or one of your own choosing and list key cultural intelligence, protocols or practices that a New Zealand exporter needs to consider.

South Korea	Japan	Indonesia
Saudi Arabia	Singapore	Malaysia
Nigeria	Samoa	

_____

_____

_____

_____

_____

example

BusinessNZ is committed to New Zealand's success — sustainable growth through free enterprise.

Advocating for enterprise and promoting the voice of thousands of businesses across New Zealand, we work for positive change through new thinking, productivity and innovation.

Our unique strength lies in our capability to engage with government officials, community groups, MPs and Ministers on a daily basis, ensuring business interests are represented throughout the policy-making process.

What we do affects all New Zealanders, because when business is going well, it affects the wellbeing of our economy, our environment, our jobs, our communities, our families and our futures.

tasks

4   a   BusinessNZ advocates businesses going well is good for our economy and our environment. Explain why this statement is true, using examples.

_____

_____

_____

_____

_____

_____

b   Discuss with your classmates and teacher as to why such a group as BusinessNZ is needed 'to engage with government officials', etc. List what policies might BusinessNZ want to lobby against. Hint: check www.businessnz.org.nz and the Business Issues section, in particular the Employment Relations and Export and Trade sections.

_____

_____

_____

_____

_____

c   BusinessNZ is the promoter of the Buy NZ Made campaign. Owned and run by BusinessNZ, the Buy NZ Made campaign began in 1988. The campaign is a non-government-run initiative created by the Manufacturers Federation, now Business NZ. Its mission is to keep New Zealand working by promoting and supporting the manufacturing, exporting and retailing of New Zealand-made goods.

What value would this campaign have for New Zealand exporters expanding into international markets?

_____

_____

_____

_____

_____

d   What aspects of New Zealand would a New Zealand exporter want to promote versus overseas competition, for example selling New Zealand-made products into China, India or the USA?

_____

_____

_____

_____

_____

_____

e   Find out what services BusinessNZ can specifically offer to help a New Zealand business looking to expand overseas, and list four key areas of assistance.

_____

_____

_____

_____

_____

_____

_____

ISBN: 9780170352598

f   How much does BusinessNZ membership cost?

_____

_____

Angel investors versus venture capitalists

A venture capitalist is an investor who either provides capital to startup ventures or supports small companies that wish to expand but do not have access to traditional sources of finance. Venture capitalists are willing to invest in such companies because they can earn a massive return on their investments if these companies are a success. Think Facebook, eBay, app developers.

An angel investor is an investor who provides financial backing for small startups or entrepreneurs and is usually found among an entrepreneur's family and friends. The capital they provide can be a one-time injection finance or ongoing support to carry the company through difficult times. Angel investors give more favourable terms than other lenders, as they are usually investing in the person rather than the viability of the business. They are focused on helping the business succeed, rather than reaping a huge profit from their investment.

Angel investors are essentially the exact opposite of a venture capitalist.

tasks

5   a   Go online and view an episode of *Dragon's Den* (from any country!) or *Shark Tank*. Are the Dragons/ Sharks featured on the programmes angel investors or venture capitalists? Explain your answer.

_____

_____

_____

_____

_____

b   New Zealand has an Angel Association (www.angelassociation.co.nz). List the two main objectives of this association, and two services it provides to New Zealand businesses.

_____

_____

_____

_____

_____

_____

_____

_____

case study

Rockit apples

What are Rockit apples?

You won't find Rockit apples in a wooden bin in the produce section of your local supermarket. Launched in 2010, the fruit are marketed as a healthy snack on-the-run and come in plastic cylinders of three, four or five apples. The packaging is designed to be stacked at a checkout counter and inside the cup holder of a car or golf trundler. Slightly bigger than a golf ball, the New Zealand-grown variety looks and tastes like a normal apple.

Originally developed by Crown research organisation Plant and Food Research (PFR), the Havelock North Fruit Company bought the global rights to the Rockit cultivar in 2002. When competitors were trying to grow larger apples, Rockit saw an opportunity to turn people back to fruit as a snack rather than confectionery.

It takes two years for a Rockit tree to produce fruit, and seven years for the trees to reach full capacity. To speed up expansion, the Havelock North Fruit Company has raised $9 million in capital, including seed funding from the New Zealand Venture Investment Fund (NZVIF). Tauranga angel investment group, Enterprise Angels, also contributed more than $4 million in four funding rounds.

6 a Complete the table on Rockit apples below. We suggest you start at their website, www.rockitapple.com.

Where is the business located?	
What is the product?	
What is the company's point of difference versus competitors?	
In your view, why is it successful?	

Who is Phil Alison?	
Would Rockit apples use BusinessNZ? How?	
Would Rockit apples be attractive to angel investors or venture capitalists?	

b Finally, explain why this type of investment is good for the business *and* New Zealand.

_____

_____

_____

_____

_____

_____

_____

_____

_____

_____

_____

_____

_____

_____

_____

_____

_____

_____

_____

_____

unit 3

Apply business knowledge to address a complex problem (or problems) in a given global business context.

Students are expected to apply knowledge to address problems arising from the following:

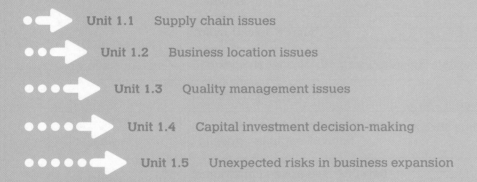

Unit 1.1 Supply chain issues

Unit 1.2 Business location issues

Unit 1.3 Quality management issues

Unit 1.4 Capital investment decision-making

Unit 1.5 Unexpected risks in business expansion

For the external exam: Candidates will be expected to refer to an actual example of a New Zealand-registered business operating in a global context that they have studied during the year for 3.1 and 3.2. **However, this standard uses a resource booklet that candidates are expected to use, refer to, and comment on in their answers.**

The key concepts (enterprise, globalisation, citizenship, and sustainability) and the Māori concepts (pūtake, tūranga, tikanga, kaitiakitanga, and rangatiratanga) are relevant to all achievement standards and should be incorporated in student answers whenever possible.

Māori concepts that relate to business may be assessed. Where this occurs, students will be **given a definition or explanation of the term** in the examination paper, and they will be required to apply or explain the concept in relation to a specific business context. Therefore, the more you know your business, the better you will be positioned to relate to the Māori concept.

For this standard, 90381 (3.3), students will be required to fully **explain the causes** and **effects of the problem, suggest solutions**, and make a fully **justified recommendation**.

Candidates will be **expected to refer to the given context** provided in the resource material.

How to construct an examination answer

In simple terms, **why** might the problem have occurred, **what** has been the effect on the business, **how** could the business fix the problem (TWO possible solutions at least), and explain **why you would recommend one of those solutions** as the best option. The marker will be looking for an **additional**, significant reason in the recommendation from the two solutions provided for Excellence. If you just repeat the solution, you will be limiting your grade to Merit.

Therefore in planning your answer, ensure you have TWO solutions with at least one significant reason for each solution (preferably TWO), plus one of the solutions with **ANOTHER** reason. Your answer doesn't necessarily need to be right, only **justified**.

The model for your answer:

Achieved

Why might the problem have occurred, and impact on the business (often related to increased costs, loss of profit, impact of sales/brand/customers?

Option 1

Describe and explain what and why.

Merit

Option 2

Describe and explain what and why.

Option 1/2 is the best solution because ... (**new reason** in addition to that already provided). Overall this option will be the most beneficial to the business by ... (impact of sales/revenue/costs/profits /marker share etc) on the business.

Merit plus Excellence

  ISBN: 9780170352598

3.1 Supply chain issues

What is a **supply chain**?

A supply chain is all the stages in the production **sequence** (hence the term 'chain', meaning each part is linked to the stage before and after) that converts raw materials into a product/service purchased by consumers. It comprises businesses that supply raw materials, producers who convert the raw material into products, warehouses that store the semi-finished or finished products, distribution centres that deliver to the retailers, and retailers who present the product to the final user: everything that is involved from origin to point of consumption.

Why is the supply chain important?

Consider a simple example: making ballpoint pens. The producer/manufacturer will constantly be assessing how it makes pens and tries to reduce costs wherever possible so that the product is competitive to the retailers and to market. However, if the supply chain has issues such as shipping delays, damage in transit, warehouse damage or theft, then the inefficiency of the supply chain makes the product (pens in this case) uncompetitive. A poor supply chain adds costs. An efficient (no waste such as time) supply chain minimises costs, and therefore can make the product be more competitive.

Consider another example: in summer, how would a dairy that sells ice cream perform if the freezers at the local distribution centre suffered a 48-hour power outage? The dairy may not be able to get fresh supplies of ice cream, and therefore could lose sales against a competitor dairy if they were able to source ice cream from another distribution centre. In this case, it's not the producer at fault, nor the dairy, but the supply chain that impacts on the supply of product to the end user, the consumer.

Key terms

Outsourcing: A business may consider it better to focus on its key strengths rather than perform all its business activities, and outsource (or 'contract out') an activity by using independent suppliers rather than undertaking the work itself. For example, a business may choose to contract out or outsource its legal, IT or accounting work to another company.

Distribution: The movement of a good or service from the producer to the end user through a 'distribution channel'. For example, a product made in Blenheim will have a vastly different distribution channel from a product made in China, including different freight options, length of time for freight, volume able to be moved and insurance risk.

Procurement: The process of buying goods and services for the business. The ability of a business to buy the right product or service at the right time and price can be critical to the sustainability of the business. For example, a juice producer that is unable to source fruit to process at a competitive rate will be uncompetitive in the market.

ISBN: 9780170352598

In a business, the two functions of distribution and procurement may be standalone functions of a department or individual, such as a distribution manager or procurement manager, as these are recognised as important functions to the success of the business.

Example of a distribution chain

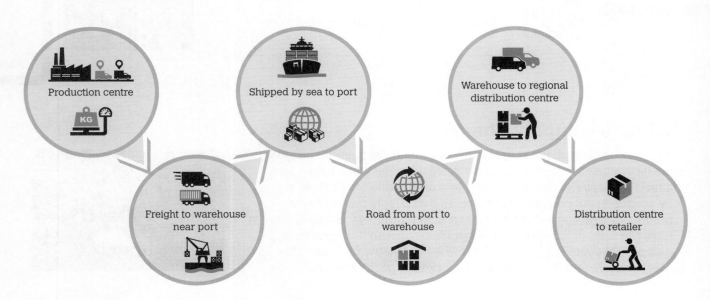

tasks

1   With reference to a New Zealand-registered business:

a   Explain the role distribution has on the success of the business.

_____

_____

_____

b   What would be the impact in a major breakdown in the distribution channel? Explain.

_____

_____

_____

c   Explain the role procurement has on the success of the business.

_____

_____

_____

   ISBN: 9780170352598

d What would be the impact of a significant cost increase in a major component to the business? Explain.

_____

_____

_____

_____

_____

2 Map a distribution channel for one of the businesses you have studied. Identify where major inputs come from, where the major production takes place, the various freight issues the business would use to bring the inputs together and the finished product to market, the role of warehouses, distribution centres, etc. In addition, at every stage, identify what language would be predominantly used, what cultural and legal implications might be involved, and suggest how these could impact on the performance of the distribution channel. If one of your businesses is not suitable, consider the supply channel of Tip Top ice cream to Saudi Arabia and Cuba.

_____

_____

_____

_____

_____

_____

_____

_____

_____

_____

_____

_____

_____

_____

_____

3 Using your map of the distribution channels, from task 2, how complex is it? What issues could seriously impact on its performance?

_____

_____

_____

_____

_____

ISBN: 9780170352598

4   What value does a warehouse offer to a business distributing products across the world?

_____

_____

_____

_____

_____

_____

5   Identify a business that uses few intermediaries such as warehouses or freight channels. What does this suggest for competitiveness?

_____

_____

_____

_____

_____

_____

_____

6   Sketch out a channel from a dairy farm to the supply of milk powder in central China. What role do freight efficiencies have on the cost structure to supply milk powder to a Chinese retailer?

_____

_____

_____

_____

_____

_____

_____

_____

7   Why would lowest cost of freight not be regarded as the best choice for a New Zealand-based business exporting to an overseas market? What other factors might be more important than cost?

_____

_____

_____

_____

_____

_____

   ISBN: 9780170352598

8   NCEA-style question.

Deadly China blast disrupts world's 10th largest port

SHANGHAI (AP) Explosions that sent huge fireballs through China's Tianjin port have disrupted the flow of cars, oil, iron ore and other items through the world's 10th largest port.

The blast sent shipping containers tumbling into one another, leaving them in bent, charred piles. Rows of new cars, lined up on vast lots for distribution across China, were reduced to blackened carcasses.

Ships carrying oil and 'hazardous products' were barred from the port on Thursday, the Tianjin Maritime Safety Administration said on its official microblog. It also said vessels were not allowed to enter the central port zone, which is near the blast site.

Tianjin is the 10th largest port in the world by container volume and the seventh largest in China, according to the World Shipping Council, moving more containers than the ports of Rotterdam, Hamburg and Los Angeles.

Australian mining giant BHP Billiton said the blast had disrupted iron ore shipments and port operations, but had not damaged any iron ore at the port. 'We are working with our customers to minimise any potential impact,' it said in a statement on Thursday.

Volkswagen spokeswoman Larissa Braun said vehicles at a storage facility near the blast were damaged. 'We will ship cars from our storage facilities at other ports to ensure our dealers have adequate supply,' she said.

Danish shipping and oil group A.P. Moller-Maersk said operations at its Tianjin port terminals, which are 5 kilometres (3 miles) from the blast site, resumed on Thursday. A few warehouses owned and operated by suppliers to its logistics company, Damco, were damaged, two of them seriously.

Tianjin is northern China's largest port, a gateway to Beijing that has grown in importance as companies seeking lower manufacturing costs migrated from China's eastern and southeastern manufacturing centres. Motorola, Toyota, Samsung, Nestlé, Honeywell, Coca-Cola, Bridgestone, Lafarge, GlaxoSmithKline and Novo Nordisk, among others, have operations in Tianjin, according to a government trade promotion website.

The overall economic impact of the blast will hinge, in part, on how long the clean-up takes. The government has so far said little about the cause of the blast. Tianjin authorities suspended firefighting on Thursday so chemical experts could survey for hazardous materials and the local Environmental Protection Bureau said it had identified toluene and chloroform in the air. Sean Liu, general manager of ICIS China, a commodities research firm, said preliminary interviews with companies at the port suggested that the near-term economic impact for most industries would likely be muted. But he said the blast could have long-term implications for the cost structure of China's energy and petrochemicals industry, if the government imposes stricter supply chain safety standards.

a   Fully explain the **causes** and **effects** of the decision to close the Tianjin port for three days on one of the companies based in China such as Toyota.

_____

_____

_____

_____

_____

_____

_____

_____

_____

_____

_____

b   Suggest TWO possible **solutions** to address the problem of the port being closed for that company.

i   _____

_____

_____

_____

ii   _____

_____

_____

c   Evaluate how the two possible **solutions** you named in b would address the problem of the port closure and disruption to supply chain and make a **fully justified recommendation**. In your answer, you should:

   •   fully explain the advantages and disadvantages that each solution has for the business and its stakeholders

   •   state the solution that you would recommend.

_____

_____

_____

_____

_____

_____

_____

_____

_____

d Justify your recommendation by explaining why this recommendation is better than the other possible solution.

_____

Remember: The recommendation should start 'Option 1 (or 2) is the better option because …' and add in a statement NOT used in your evaluation. You need to carefully structure the answer to ensure you have a distinct point to make (in addition to previous points) in the recommendation. So draft your answer before writing it in full.

ISBN: 9780170352598

3.2 Business location issues

Location, location, location!

How important will this decision be for a business, and who should make it? Is it an operational decision, where the factory should be located based on availability of resources such as labour? Or is it a marketing decision based on access to markets? Or a financial decision based on maximising profits?

For existing businesses, location decisions are often associated with moving — to a new location with better resources, access to transport or infrastructure, or a change in scale of operation requiring smaller or larger facilities. In this case, change management is a key factor, as the impact on staff may be significant, such as moving a factory from Levin to Westport.

For a new business, location will be a balance of two factors:

1 **Quantitative factors**: the financial measures of the site including cost of land, labour, transport, building costs or possible local/state government support subsidies. Quantitative means we can have a value or 'quantity' of dollars with each factor. These factors are used to determine **return on investment, breakeven analysis and payback period**.

2 **Qualitative factors**: the non-measureable factors that may influence a business decision, such as the owner's or manager's preference, ethical considerations (such as staying in New Zealand or moving to Mexico), quality of infrastructure, environmental concerns including adverse publicity because of new development in a sensitive environmental area, and potential room for expansion.

 ISBN: 9780170352598

tasks

Assess the following tasks using quantitative factors.

1   JAF Hair Products is planning to open four more shops, two in New Zealand and two in Australia. JAF has borrowed a large amount of money for the expansion, and while interest rates are relatively low, it appears there may be an increase coming in the next year. Consider the data below, and evaluate which sites you would recommend expanding to.

a   Which sites would you recommend to JAF, and why? Ensure you show some calculations.

	NZ sites — cost of site/ building NZ$2 million	Australian sites — cost of site/ building NZ$3 million
Length of time to repay money borrowed for expansion (payback period)	2.5 years	3.8 years
Annual profit made as % of initial cost	12%	14%

_____
_____
_____
_____
_____
_____

b   What quantitative factors might be important as well?

_____
_____
_____
_____
_____
_____
_____
_____

2 Speedy Manure Systems operates a highly effective waste process.
They are looking at two possible locations, one in Auckland and another
in Kaharoa, near Rotorua.

a Calculate the estimated annual profits for the two locations.

	Auckland site	Kaharoa site
Estimated annual costs	$980,000	$500,000
Forecast annual sales (units)	25,000	17,000
Forecast selling price per unit	$50	$45

b Why might the annual profits change in future years? Hint: Which location would expect its costs to
rise more than the other and why?

3 Complete the right-hand column of the table using a business you have studied, or choose one of the
following to research.

Fisher & Paykel   Macpac   3M New Zealand   Xero   Hapara

Business location	Evidence and explanation
Reasons for locating the whole business overseas or a specific unit (such as production of a particular product)	

Why is the location so important for the following?	
Customers	
Suppliers	
Infrastructure	
Transport	
Resources	
Competitive advantage	
Trade agreements	

4   a   Look up the term 'clustering'. Explain what it is, and give a specific example of clustering in your local area. Hint: Consider where automotive trade businesses are located, entertainment/fast-food businesses and/or medical/dental services.

_____

_____

_____

_____

_____

ISBN: 9780170352598

b   List two advantages and two disadvantages of clustering for any business looking to expand overseas.

Advantages of clustering	Disadvantages of clustering

c   Consider a global company operating in New Zealand. Where might be the top three locations chosen to set up in New Zealand?

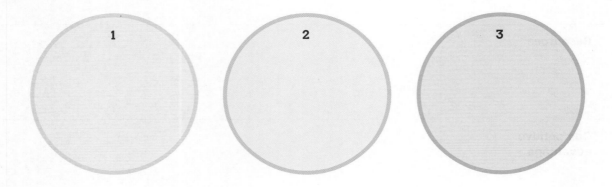

d   Consider a New Zealand-registered business developing innovative gaming software looking to locate part of its operation (such as a sales/marketing or programming department) overseas. Which three most likely locations in the world might it choose? Justify your answer.

	Location	Justification
1		
2		
3		

Locating an operation overseas

Why would a business choose to locate some or all of its operations in another country? The following are key reasons.

Reduce costs	A clear favourite to justify relocation, particularly relocating a labour intensive production activity to low-wage economies such as India, Malaysia or Eastern Europe. Reduced costs may translate into increased profits and returns for shareholders.
Access to new or growing markets	Many businesses have looked at the rapid growth of individual wealth in the Middle East, Thailand, Malaysia, Singapore, South Korea and China. Higher individual wealth usually corresponds with increased demand for a wider range of consumer products.
To avoid protectionist or restrictive trade practices	Where a barrier exists for the sale of goods within a country, many businesses will set up in a country which bypasses the barrier. An example is the location of car assembly plants in some countries such as China and Mexico.
To gain governmental support	Local and national governments may subsidise some location costs such as low-interest loans, tax breaks or 'free' land to support the location costs within that country. Ireland, Queensland and New Zealand have all been active in this way. (Remember the debate about tax incentives to encourage *The Hobbit* to be filmed here?)
Access to resources	Many countries have developed high-quality labour such as engineers, doctors and materials scientists that attract companies requiring those skills to locate. China, India and Thailand are all examples.
Exchange rate volatility	Locating a production facility within a country to produce products for that country is one way to avoid the exchange rate highs and lows of supplying from outside the country. All costs, sales and taxes are in local currency.

Potential issues when locating overseas

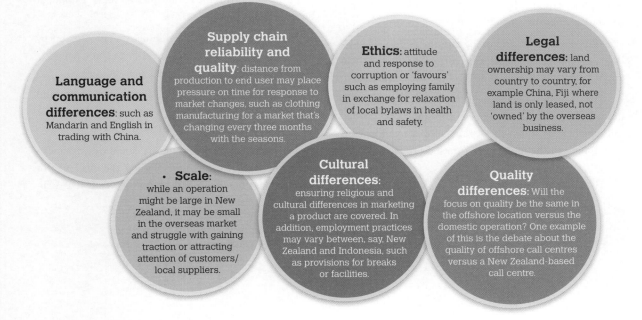

Language and communication differences: such as Mandarin and English in trading with China.

Supply chain reliability and quality: distance from production to end user may place pressure on time for response to market changes, such as clothing manufacturing for a market that's changing every three months with the seasons.

Ethics: attitude and response to corruption or 'favours' such as employing family in exchange for relaxation of local bylaws in health and safety.

Legal differences: land ownership may vary from country to country, for example China, Fiji where land is only leased, not 'owned' by the overseas business.

- **Scale:** while an operation might be large in New Zealand, it may be small in the overseas market and struggle with gaining traction or attracting attention of customers/local suppliers.

Cultural differences: ensuring religious and cultural differences in marketing a product are covered. In addition, employment practices may vary between, say, New Zealand and Indonesia, such as provisions for breaks or facilities.

Quality differences: Will the focus on quality be the same in the offshore location versus the domestic operation? One example of this is the debate about the quality of offshore call centres versus a New Zealand-based call centre.

tasks

5   NCEA-style question.

Western China ripe for business opportunities

Abulaiti Aijinmaiti shrugs when asked about the spectacular sharemarket crash that has become a major talking point among China's middle class.

Of much greater importance for Aijinmaiti, an ethnic Uighur, are the grapes that hang heavily on the vines outside, ready for the harvest, which is a major source of income in the oasis town set among the sands of the Taklamakan Desert.

But the country's vast, sparsely populated western regions — which also include Tibet, Sichuan, Qinghai and Yunnan — are on the rise, thanks to Government investment and policies introduced over the past 15 years aimed at closing the development gap. That growth is now creating opportunities for some New Zealand companies.

In 2013, Chinese president Xi Jinping announced the Silk Road Economic Belt strategy, which includes a push to build a network of high-speed railway lines, roads and pipelines across western China.

The central Government is also pushing to urbanise the west in the hope of creating more consumers — a key plank in the country's efforts to re-balance the economy towards domestic consumption. In Jiaohe Town, for example, there are plans to build 180 houses for the resettlement of rural families.

'Our economy is developing rapidly,' Aijinmaiti says. 'We have subsidies for planting cotton, building houses and also for animal husbandry and medical insurance.'

The central Government is also pushing to industrialise Xinjiang by establishing 20 special industrial zones across the region, similar to those that contributed to the rapid rise of coastal provinces in the late 20th century.

The development push in the west is opening up fresh opportunities for New Zealand companies at a time when China's overall economic growth is slowing.

Auckland-based freight and logistics operator Mainfreight recently opened a branch in Chengdu, capital of the southwestern Sichuan province.

Managing director Don Braid says the company set up shop in Chengdu in response to the westward move of industry.

'What might have been — five or ten years ago — small cities, have become large manufacturing areas,' Braid says. 'Manufacturers have moved west to take advantage of cheaper labour and tax subsidies and other incentives from regional governments to attract business to their area. For us, in logistics, we need to be in those regions.'

The transit time, at 15 days, is about 11 days faster than sea freight, he says.

However, Simon Page, managing director of New Zealand infant formula exporter and retailer Biopure Health, says Kiwi firms are failing to make the most of the business opportunities in western China.

His company has been operating New Zealand Milk Bar retail stores in Sichuan for several years and opened a flagship outlet in Chengdu, the provincial capital, at the weekend.

It is the company's 30th Chinese retail site and by next year it aims to have 100 outlets. Page says Chengdu's retail market has been developing rapidly.

'Starbucks is on just about every corner now and they're all busy,' he says. 'That's a really good sign that you've got middle-class consumers.'

However, Page adds there are some drawbacks to doing business in the west, including the challenge of serving consumers who can be less sophisticated than those further east.

a   Perceived advantages of locating a business in western China have resulted in an influx of New Zealand businesses. Explain ONE factor that might encourage a New Zealand food producer to locate a branch or facility there.

_____

_____

_____

_____

_____

b   Fully explain the impact on Mainfreight of locating a branch in Chengdu by explaining ONE advantage and ONE disadvantage of this strategy.

_____

_____

_____

_____

_____

_____

c   Evaluate in detail an international location of a New Zealand-registered business you have studied in depth. In your answer, you should:

   •   describe the business and the international location where it decided to set up its overseas operation
   •   fully explain TWO advantages of the location
   •   fully explain TWO disadvantages of the location
   •   draw conclusions on which are the most significant factors in making the decision about location.

> Name of New Zealand registered business:
>
> _____

_____

_____

_____

_____

_____

_____

_____

_____

6   a   If you had a choice of country to work in, assuming you were paid the same amount in salary wherever you choose, where would it be? Why?

_____

_____

_____

_____

b   If you had to go to either Colombia, Papua New Guinea or Chad, discuss the qualitative factors you would consider.

_____

_____

_____

_____

_____

c   What qualitative factors bring people to New Zealand?

_____

_____

_____

_____

_____

_____

d   What quantitative factors are not so attractive for New Zealand?

_____

_____

_____

_____

_____

_____

_____

3.3 Quality management issues

Quality management ensures that an organisation, product or service is consistent.

Quality management has four principal components:

1 Quality planning
2 Quality control
3 Quality assurance
4 Quality improvement.

Quality planning

What is going to be made, when, with what resources and inputs, by what date, etc. The planning will detail the steps the process of producing the product will take and the timeframe.

Quality control

The activities employed in checking the output due to the production system, and measures to solve any defects found. Usually checking after the good or service has been produced, thus incurring all costs to date. Often quoted as QC.

Quality assurance

Often incorrectly used in place of quality control, quality assurance is a wider concept that covers all policies and systematic activities within a quality system. Therefore checks on quality are at every stage of the production system, including design and testing of suppliers' products, not just at the final stage when all costs have been incurred.

Quality improvement

The systematic approach to a reduction or the elimination of waste, rework, and losses in the production process. This is often an ongoing process, as the business seeks to remove costs from wasteful production while maintaining or improving the final product's quality.

Why is quality management important?

As businesses compete for consumers' attention, production is constantly reviewed to take costs out and have a competitively-priced good or service in the market. If the good has faults and is judged by consumers to be of lesser quality than similarly-priced products, then consumers will choose the higher quality product/service.

Therefore quality management is what will keep a business in the market, making it sustainable.

ISBN: 9780170352598

tasks

Research the following areas of quality management.

CONTINUOUS IMPROVEMENT →

1   Total quality management (TQM): what is it, and in particular, how does it involve employees of a company?

_____

_____

_____

_____

_____

_____

2   Benchmarking: what is it and why would a business do it?

_____

_____

_____

_____

3   If you were running a chicken farm, what business might you benchmark against? Why?

_____

_____

_____

4   Kaizen: what is it and what relevance does it have to quality?

_____

_____

_____

_____

5   What are quality circles? What business is most famous for them, and why?

_____

_____

_____

_____

_____

6   What is LEAN manufacturing? Explain the term, and give an example of its application in a factory making microwaves or similar products.

_____

_____

_____

_____

_____

7   Define the three most common methods of production — job, batch, and mass/continuous production — and provide a clear example of each type.

_____

_____

_____

_____

_____

_____

_____

Now evaluate quality management with the following questions.

8   Why might a restaurant that buys in only top-quality products still be classed as providing poor-quality meals by customers?

_____

_____

_____

_____

9   If good quality keeps a business sustainable, what does poor quality do? Explain with reference to price, and the impact on the business.

_____

_____

_____

_____

10 How could a quality management system lower total costs for a business?

_____

_____

_____

_____

11 What role does quality play in the following companies? Investigate the websites for statements regarding the quality of their products.

Business	Reason for failure
hp	
AIR NEW ZEALAND	
Heinz	
3M	
Fonterra Dairy for life	
TOYOTA	
Nestlé	
the warehouse	

   ISBN: 9780170352598

12 What role do employees have in the pursuit of higher quality in a business?

_____

_____

_____

_____

_____

_____

13 a Investigate the following quality initiatives.

Quality initiative	Brief description
Six Sigma	
Quality Circles	
Kaizen (continuous improvement)	
Zero defects	
Benchmarking	

ISBN: 9780170352598

b   Identify which quality initiatives (if any) the businesses you have studied this year use and why.

_____

_____

_____

_____

_____

_____

_____

_____

_____

14 Give two marketing advantages that come from a quality reputation.

_____

_____

_____

_____

_____

_____

_____

_____

15 Discuss in groups, then formulate a response to the following statement: 'Quality management is solely an issue for the production team.'

_____

_____

_____

_____

_____

_____

_____

_____

_____

_____

_____

_____

_____

   ISBN: 9780170352598

Capital investment decision-making

This section deals with the decisions the business may make in regard to investments. These investments could include the purchase of new vehicles or new buildings, or the relocation to a new city, state or possibly a new country. While all of these are of significant cost and impact on the business, other investments may be of a smaller scale such as decisions on replacement of a phone system, printer or office furniture.

What are capital goods?

These are any assets in an organisation that are tangible (that you can touch) and which are used to produce other goods or services, for example office buildings and equipment and machinery. To a builder, a hammer is a capital good but a hammer sold to a consumer (a home handy person or student) is NOT a capital good. It's the use of the good (to make another good for further production or to make the final consumer good) that makes it a capital good.

How do we go about making these decisions?

The business term is called investment appraisal, which means the evaluation of the profitability or desirability of an investment project.

There are two methods of the investment appraisal:

1 **Quantitative factors** in investment appraisal, by using numbers such as time, costs, and interest rates to assist in determining the investment project.	2 **Qualitative factors** in investment appraisal, which are the more intangible aspects that may impact on a decision. These may include such things as impact on the community or the environment, risks around getting legal approvals for the project, confidence in the data, management appetite for risk, and, lastly, the alignment with the objectives of the business. In this last instance, this could involve a business not pursuing a decision on replacing workers with new technology when one business objective is the development of staff and relationships with customers.

The key quantitative factors are:

1   **Payback period**: the length of time it takes for the net cash inflows to pay back the original capital cost of the investment. The payment method is often used as it is quick, simple to calculate, and useful as a means of comparing projects. It is, however, generally used with other methods, not on its own.

> For example: a company invests $400,000 in a new machine. The cash saving from the new machine is expected to be $100,000/year for 10 years. **The payback period is therefore 4 years:**
>
> $$\frac{\$400,000}{\$100,000} \text{ per year}$$

2   **Average rate of return (ARR)**: this measures the annual profitability of an investment as a percentage of the initial investment, and is a simple calculation:

> $$ARR = \frac{\text{annual profit (net cash flow)}}{\text{initial capital cost}} \times \frac{100}{1}$$

The advantage of ARR is that it focuses on profitability, can compare with other projects and can be quickly assessed. However, this method also doesn't take into account the payback period, hence it needs to be used in conjunction with that other method. It also ignores the time value of money.

3   **Discounted payback**: similar to average rate of return but incorporating the time value of money. What this means is that the impacts of interest rates in time are included. For example, $1000 received today would equal $1000. However, if I promise to pay you $1000 in one year, what will actually be the value of that $1000 when I hand you that cash? We all know that the $1000, if we received it today and placed it in a bank, may have a value of $1100 in a year depending on the rate of interest. In other words, $1100 in one year may be equal to $1000 today at 10%.

4   **Net present value (NPV)**: this method works on what today's value of the estimated cash flows would be from an investment. This method also uses discounted cash flows but subtracts them from the capital cost to give NPV. The advantage of NPV is that the rate of discount can be altered if economic circumstances are expected to change. The disadvantage is that it's reasonably complex to work out, and any inaccuracy in forecasting interest rates may build an inaccurate answer.

tasks

Payback period

1   a   Calculate the payback period for the following.

Sages Beer Shop requires an investment of $200,000 and it generates cash as follows:

$20,000 in Year 1 $100,000 in Year 4

$60,000 in Year 2 $70,000 in Year 5

$80,000 in Year 3

The payback period is _____ years.

Hint: $20,000 + $60,000 + $80,000 = $160,000 in the first three years + $40,000 (of the $100,000 occurring in Year 4).

b Milnes Homes is planning to undertake a project requiring initial investment of $50 million and is expected to generate $10 million in Year 1, $13 million in Year 2, $16 million in Year 3, $19 million in Year 4 and $22 million in Year 5. Calculate the payback value of the project.

Cumulative		
(cash flows in millions)		
Year	**Cash flow**	**Cash flow**
0	(50)	(50)
1	10	(40)
2	13	(27)
3	16	(11)
4	19	8
5	22	30

Calculations: _____

_____

_____

Average rate of return

2 Da Vinci Studios is looking at buying a new automatic painting machine. The cost of the machine is $200,000 and the expected net cash flows are:

Year	1	2	3	4	5
Net cash flow ($)	50,000	55,000	65,000	75,000	75,000

The total return from the project over the five years is $320,000 (the total). If we subtract the original cost of $200,000, we get the net return from the investment to be $120,000. To calculate the ARR, we use the following formula:

$$\text{Average rate of return} = \frac{\text{average net cash flow}}{\text{capital cost}} \times 100$$

From the figures above, this gives us: _____

_____

_____

ISBN: 9780170352598

Discounted payback

3 Discount tables are used to help in any calculation. You should not need to carry out major calculations, but should understand the difference between payback and discounted payback, which takes into account the time value of money.

Look at the table below regarding a purchase of a major asset for $5 m today (Year 0) with interest rates at 10%. The discount factor is zero in the present, because $1 = $1; there is no loss of value over time. The cash flow is negative $5 m, as it is out of the business.

Year	Net cash flow ($m)	Discount factor	Discounted cash flow	Cumulative discounted cash flows
0	(5)	1.00	(5)	(5)
1	2	0.91	1.82	(3.18)
2	2	0.83	1.66	(1.52)
3	2	0.75	1.50	(0.02)
4	3	0.68	2.04	2.02

The table shows that in Year 3, cash inflow has almost covered the value of the investment, but not quite. In Year 4, the cumulative discounted cash flows have covered the initial investment and future cash flows will be only positive.

From the information, calculate the payback period. Show your working here:

_____

Your calculation should have been two years and six months.

The key aspect is that discount payback will always be longer than payback period because future cash has less value in today's money due to interest rates and inflation.

Net present value

Net present value (NPV) calculates the present values of all the money coming in for a project or planned investment in the future, and matches this against the money being spent. We therefore get a result which is the net present value of that project or planned investment. The key advantage is that it allows us to compare NPV results across different projects/investments, and therefore make a decision on the best financial return. Projects are only worth carrying out if the NPV is positive, and it is often compared with the rate of return if the money stayed invested in a bank or financial institution. For example, an NPV of 5% versus current interest rates of 7% may not see the project proceed, as the financial return is better if the money stays in the bank.

For those with a knowledge of economics, NPV takes the opportunity cost of money into account — what the next best alternative is. Unfortunately, NPV is a little complex to calculate and the result is often misunderstood.

4 Reynolds Doughnuts has decided that an investment will be carried out if they meet the following criteria:

Payback	30 months
Average rate of return	18%
Net present value	10% of the investment outlay

The doughnut production section has suggested purchasing a $600,000 machine, which will increase productivity and quality. Estimates of output gains should produce the following cash flow over the four-year life of the machine.

Year 0	−$600,000	Discount factor
Year 1	+$130,000	0.91
Year 2	+$260,000	0.83
Year 3	+$360,000	0.75
Year 4	+$230,000	0.68

Additional information: the machine will be able to be sold for $100,000 at the end of the fourth year.

a   Using the information above, conduct an investment appraisal for Reynolds Doughnuts.

_____

_____

_____

_____

_____

_____

_____

b   Outline any other information that might be useful for Reynolds Doughnuts in making its decision.

_____

_____

_____

c   Explain the purpose of discounting cash flows.

_____

_____

d   How useful is payback period as the only method for making an investment decision?

_____

_____

_____

e   Where might a business go to fund an investment? Outline two sources.

_____

_____

_____

_____

_____

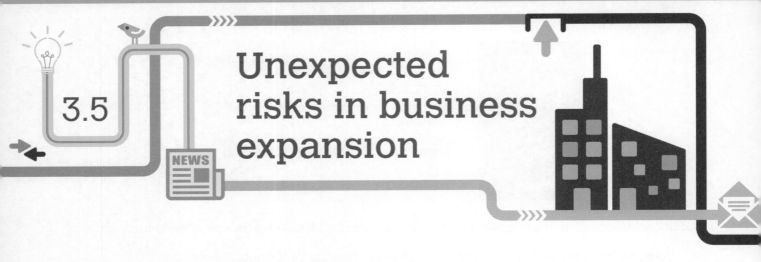

Unexpected risks in business expansion

3.5

This topic deals with the unexpected risks involved in expanding globally such as cultural and language barriers, economic uncertainty, legal regulations, and international trade agreements.

A New Zealand-registered business looking to expand globally faces risks. These risks, however, can be reduced if the business researches the overseas markets and implements strategies that identify the risks, which in turn may present solutions, and therefore makes the expansion sustainable.

Cultural and language risks: The cultural practices of a country must never be assumed to be the same in other countries. For example, drinking alcohol is accepted in New Zealand but strictly forbidden in Saudi Arabia, a major trading partner. A language example can be the translation of written text — just look at the debate around the Treaty of Waitangi English and Māori versions.

Economic risks: For example the chance that macroeconomic conditions like exchange rates, interest rates, or political stability will affect an investment. Consider the cost of a US$20,000 car four years ago, two years ago, and today (ignoring any discount factors!). What impact would a significant change in interest rate have on the business's balance sheet? And where would the loan be raised — the domestic location (New Zealand) or the expansion site (China or USA), and what are the prevailing interest rates? And what currency do you value the profit and costs in? Local currency or euros, yen, US$ or RMB?

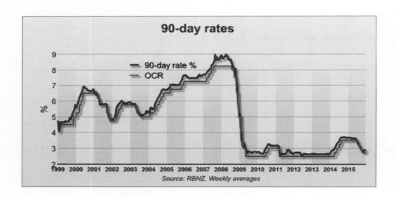

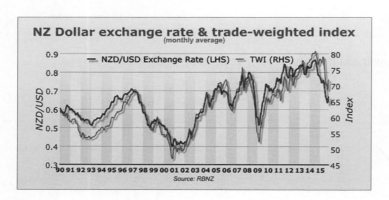

ISBN: 9780170352598

Exchange rate change and effect

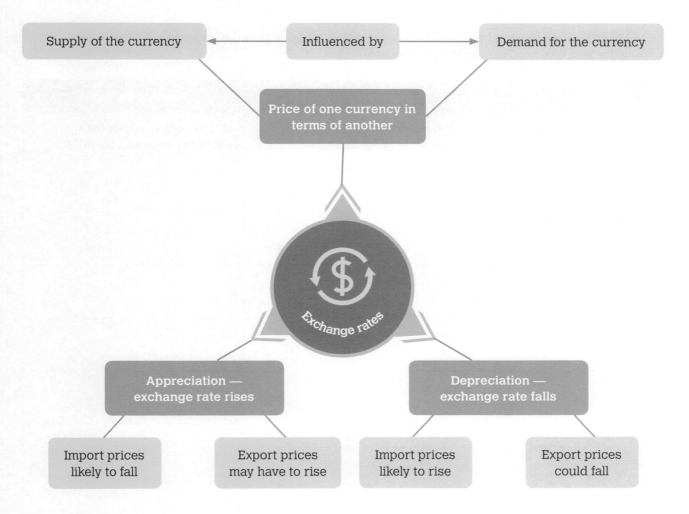

Trading environment risks: While economic risks will impact on trade through exchange rates/interest rates, other factors will also have an impact on the business. These factors could include government agreements such as New Zealand's Free Trade Agreement with China in 2008, which reduced tariffs between the two countries, biosecurity concerns (such as the recent discovery of the Queensland fruit fly), general security concerns such as war/civil unrest/terrorism, and natural disasters. All of these can influence the decision by a business to expand globally. Until recently, New Zealand businesses were subject to trade restrictions with Fiji. Consider Fonterra sales of milk powder to Iran/Iraq/Syria with the military action currently being experienced in the region.

Legal risks: New Zealand law is not international law. The rules for a business operating in this country are different to other countries and will cover such wide-ranging issues as property rights, copyright, patent protection, health and safety regulations, employment law, share trading/ownership, finance regulations, consumer laws. A business that seeks new markets overseas needs to carefully evaluate the laws and regulations for operating in that market. For example, packaging requirements regarding labelling and listing ingredients may vary from New Zealand requirements.

tasks

1 A New Zealand-registered business has decided to establish a **production** facility in Chile. What factors will the business need to consider immediately?

Factor	Impact on business	Possible solution?
E.g. distance from NZ	Freight costs for getting materials to the facility	Source locally rather than obtaining materials from NZ

2 Research the following property ownership rules for a foreign business wanting to set up in the following countries and state a key aspect:

Country	Foreign property ownership rules
China	
Fiji	
Singapore	
Saudi Arabia	

 ISBN: 9780170352598

3   A New Zealand business wants to evaluate the value of a business it owns in Singapore. To ensure all its assets across the world can be compared, it uses USD as the currency. If the business was valued at US$5 million in 2000:

a   What would its value be in US$ today?

b   What would the value have been in the following currencies in 2000 and 2015? You will need to find out the exchange rate in 2000 and 2015.

	2000	2015
US$5 million		
New Zealand $		
Australian $		
Chinese RMB		
Euros		

c   In discussion with members of your class, create a list of the most common cultural differences between two countries of your choice that would impact on a business operating overseas, for example New Zealand and Malaysia.

d   Visit the Ministry of Foreign Affairs and Trade website. What resources are available to businesses wanting to establish in another country?

e   Name three agreements currently in force and three that are being negotiated.

_____

_____

_____

_____

_____

_____

_____

4   a   Why would a business choose to access a market currently experiencing civil war, such as Syria?

_____

_____

_____

_____

b   Why would a business choose not to access such a market? List four **business** reasons.

_____

_____

_____

_____

_____

5   A business recently needed to arrange a conference call between three key staff. One was based in Miami, USA, another in Perth, Australia, and the last was in Taupo, New Zealand. Find a **convenient** time for the three to have the conference call, and list the time for each participant.

Location	Local time
Miami, USA	
Perth, Australia	
Taupo, NZ	

6   If a New Zealand business was wanting to sell soft drinks in South Australia, what legal requirement must it have on the label of the bottle or can?

_____

_____

_____

7   What has been the change in trade (value) with China since the Free Trade Agreement was signed? Research what are the main commodities New Zealand exports to China, and China exports to New Zealand.

_____

_____

_____

_____

8   If you were operating a New Zealand business making any product, what would be your concern with a free trade agreement?

_____

_____

_____

_____

9   Research the legal minimum wage in the following countries:

Country	Legal minimum wage	Convert to NZ$ as of today
Australia		
Malaysia		
Vietnam		
USA		
Hong Kong		
Fiji		
United Kingdom		
Germany		
Singapore		
Russia		

ISBN: 9780170352598

10 Explain how a company such as Whittaker's or Mojo Coffee might benefit from the signing of a free trade agreement with India.

_____

_____

_____

_____

_____

_____

_____

_____

_____

11 Fisher & Paykel moved some of its manufacturing to Mexico a few years ago. Why? Research and evaluate if this was a good business decision. Justify your answer.

_____

_____

_____

_____

_____

_____

_____

_____

_____

_____

_____

_____

_____

12 Why are New Zealanders moving back from Australia to New Zealand?

_____

_____

_____

_____

_____

_____

 ISBN: 9780170352598

_____

_____

_____

13 Consider the following mistakes in advertising.

Clairol	A hair products company, Clairol, introduced the 'Mist Stick', a curling iron, into Germany only to find out that '*mist*' is slang for manure. Not too many people had use for the manure stick to use with hair.
General Motors	'Body by Fisher', boasted the auto giant General Motors. 'Corpse by Fisher' was how the Belgians read it on the posters and media.
KFC	In Chinese, the Kentucky Fried Chicken slogan 'finger-lickin' good' came out as 'eat your fingers off'.
	A famous drug company marketed a new remedy in the United Arab Emirates. To avoid any mistakes, they used pictures. The first picture on the left was of someone ill, the next picture showed the person taking the medication, the last picture showed them looking well. What they overlooked was that in the Arab world, people read from right to left.
Schweppes Tonic Water	A campaign for Schweppes Tonic Water translated the name into Schweppes Toilet Water.
Pepsi	Original line for promotion: 'Come alive with Pepsi!' Translation: 'Pepsi brings your ancestors back from the dead!' in Chinese.
Coors beer	Coors had a brand slogan that was 'Turn it loose', however the translation came out as 'You will suffer from diarrhoea'.

a Can you find any more examples, either in cultural misunderstanding or by translation errors?

_____

_____

_____

_____

_____

_____

b Choose one of the mistakes above, and outline the impact the error may have had on the business.

_____

_____

_____

_____

_____

_____

_____

c   Now suggest two solutions for the mistake, including why the solutions would correct the mistake and position the business where it would want to be.

_____

_____

_____

_____

_____

_____

_____

_____

_____

_____

d   Which solution is the better from the two you presented in c? Explain why, without using a reason from c. That is, provide **another** reason why.

_____

_____

_____

_____

_____

_____

_____

_____

_____

_____

_____

   ISBN: 9780170352598

Exam preparation

The exam structure

Be prepared for the unexpected. The exam over the past few years has changed in structure and approach many times, so you need to be prepared to *not panic*! Whether they ask three questions with four parts or four questions with three parts, it still adds up to 12 answers that are required. The concern is which parts will contribute to your Excellence grade.

So, what are the key words?

'Explain': this does not mean describe, identify or state. It is asking you to outline in your words WHAT is happening or has happened. This will get you an Achieved.

Then you will be expected to build into that some aspects of WHY. If you have answered with a WHAT plus WHY, then you're heading for a Merit answer.

But don't stop here; consider how you can get to Excellence. If you have explained WHAT, and given some reasons WHY, then it's logical you should finish with a HOW. So your Excellence answer will incorporate what, why and how it happened. You will need to use good business language — as many business terms as you can. For example, don't say 'the business made money'; a better answer would be 'the business increased revenue, which led to increased profits'.

Tips

Build into your answer your knowledge, such as how talking about poor quality might impact on finances (decreased as consumers buy elsewhere), or intellectual property might impact on marketing of a product overseas.

Read the question carefully. What are the key words? Highlight them. What have you actually been asked to explain?

Brainstorm for a few minutes the key terms you should use in each question, then build those words into your answer.

Attempt ALL parts of ALL questions. You may pick up a single mark, which could be the difference between Not Achieved and Achieved, or Achieved and Merit, etc.

Attempting to answer three standards in three hours to Excellence level across all three is EXTREMELY difficult. Be strategic — choose two standards to spend three hours writing full, comprehensive answers that will get you Excellence. Very few students get three Excellences in one three-hour exam.

For 3.3, all the information on the business being studied will be supplied, but you are expected to bring knowledge and apply that knowledge to the business case study.

Refer to the business and people in the case study in your answers. Don't make up facts that might apply to the case study — use the facts presented and all the material supplied. It is surprising how often a fact supplied in one question can be used in other questions.

Tips

Watch YouTube or online news stories, especially for economic or business events. Why? Because it is a good source of information about business issues, and you will pick up both business knowledge and business terms.

Suggested business news sites:

www.forbes.com	www.tvnz.co.nz	www.reuters.com/news
www.stuff.co.nz	www.tv3.co.nz	
www.nzherald.co.nz	www.bbc.com	

How well do you know your New Zealand-registered business for the exam?

Complete the two tables below before proceeding into the content and activities part of this standard.

Business one: _____

Key concept	Definition	Specific example of concept
Enterprise		
Globalisation		
Citizenship		
Sustainability		

 ISBN: 9780170352598

Māori concept	Definition	Specific example of concept
Pūtake		
Tūranga		
Tikanga		
Kaitiakitanga		
Rangatiratanga		

ISBN: 9780170352598

Business two: _____

Key concept	Definition	Specific example of concept
Enterprise		
Globalisation		
Citizenship		
Sustainability		

 ISBN: 9780170352598

Māori concept	Definition	Specific example of concept
Pūtake		
Tūranga		
Tikanga		
Kaitiakitanga		
Rangatiratanga		

Complete the table with **at least one key point** against each aspect. If you don't know, find out!

Aspect	Name of business one	Name of business two
	Key point	Key point
Management:		
Name the CEO/MD		
Purpose of business		
Locations		

 ISBN: 9780170352598

Achievement Standard 3.1	Key point	Key point
Innovation — by product and/or by process.		
Identify a risk and an opportunity the business has faced.		
What corporate cultures and strategies are used to encourage innovation?		
What evidence of intellectual property management is there? Any patents, etc?		
Quality management — what system does it use (if any)? What evidence can you find?		
Change management — has the business been required to make a significant change?		
Explain what and impact.		

Achievement Standard 3.2	Key point	Key point
Identify a threat and opportunity to the business.		
List two societal expectations of the business.		
What changes in the global business environment have occurred? Name two per business.		
From the above, what was the impact on the business? What did the business do to accommodate the changes?		
Business support agencies — name three that the business may use and why.		
Cultural intelligence — explain an aspect of cultural intelligence that the business uses or needs to be aware of.		
	Key point	Key point

Achievement Standard 3.3	Key point	Key point
Describe the supply chain including outsourcing, distribution and procurement for the business.		
What business location issues have occurred or may occur?		
Have there been any quality management issues? List one at least.		
Identify a potential quality issue in pre production, during production and post production.		
Find an example of a capital investment decision. What was the outcome?		
Have there been any unexpected risks in business expansion?		

ISBN: 9780170352598

Relevant New Zealand business examples for Level 3

case study 1

Air New Zealand

Air New Zealand is an international and domestic airline group that provides air passenger and cargo transport services within New Zealand, as well as to and from Australia, the South West Pacific, Asia, North America and the United Kingdom.

Air New Zealand also encompasses business units providing engineering and ground-handling services. Subsidiaries extend to booking systems, travel wholesaling and retailing services.

The principal activity of the Air New Zealand Group is the operation of domestic and international passenger transport and cargo.

Air New Zealand Vision

'We will strive to be number one in every market we serve by creating a workplace where teams are committed to our customers in a distinctively New Zealand way, resulting in superior industry returns.'

(continued on next page)

Guiding principles

- We will be the customers' airline of choice when travelling to, from and within New Zealand.
- We will build competitive advantage in all of our businesses through the creativity and innovation of our people.
- We will champion and promote New Zealand and its people, culture and business at home and overseas.
- We will work together as a great team committed to the growth and vitality of our company and New Zealand.
- Our workplaces will be fun, energising and where everyone can make a difference.

Auckland is home to the majority of our people, with locations across the airport both Domestic and International, Engineering Technical Operations, our Contact Centre at Smales Farm on the North Shore and our Head Office in the city, which we affectionately call 'The Hub'.

Wellington and Christchurch Airports are home to the next biggest group of New Zealanders, working in the airports and engineering at Christchurch Airport. We have staff right across New Zealand under either the Air New Zealand brand or one of our subsidiary companies.

Reference Air New Zealand website: http://www.airnewzealand.co.nz/corporate-profile

Locations overseas:

China/Hong Kong	Shanghai
Japan	Tokyo, Osaka. 35 staff.
Australia	Sydney, Brisbane, Melbourne, Perth. 380 staff.
UK	London. Estimated 25 staff.
Pacific Islands	Rarotonga, Samoa, Fiji and Tahiti, Hawaii. 58 staff located in the largest centre, Rarotonga.
USA/Canada	Majority in Los Angeles. 100 staff.

Air New Zealand has great resources on its website, including the following topics as per your required standards:

Topic	Standard	Reason to investigate
Societal expectations — environmental	91380	Carbon emmisions, noise.
Societal expectations — economic	91380	Shareholder value, economic sustainability.
Cultural intelligence	91380	Link to use of haka and All Black branding to promote New Zealand as a destination.
Quality management	91379	Need for quality in engineering services, and customer experience.
Innovation — IP	91379	Air New Zealand designs new business class pod sleepers and seat designs.

Innovation – process	91379	Introduction of kiosk check-in rather than counter check-in. Plus new apps available for streamlined check-in.
Corporate culture	91379	See 'Our People' sections, sustainability section and corporate social responsibility policies.
Changes in the global marketplace	91380	The increasing tourism business for New Zealand.
Supply chain issues	91381	http://www.airnewzealand.co.nz/sustainable-sourcing
Capital investment decisions	91381	See articles regarding buying the Dreamliner planes.
Unexpected risks in expanding globally	91381	Fuel prices and the NZ:US exchange rate. Ash clouds cancel flights to Bali.

tasks

1   Tourism interest in New Zealand continues to grow, but the distance to New Zealand is still perceived as a barrier for many travellers. Give two solutions and one recommendation as to how Air New Zealand might deal with this issue.

_____

_____

_____

_____

_____

_____

2   Air New Zealand has strong competition from Jetstar in New Zealand, and airlines such as Cathay Pacific, Emirates and Qantas, all of which have much more financial resources. Provide three areas Air New Zealand could focus on as the preferred airline for visiting New Zealand.

_____

_____

_____

_____

_____

_____

case study 2

Hewlett Packard (HP) New Zealand

In 2014, the Board of Hewlett Packard (HP) announced a significant event for the global giant — from being in the world's top 20 corporations (by revenue), it would split into two separate companies that would be top 50 corporations in their own right. So on 1 November 2015, HP Inc. and Hewlett Packard Enterprise were formed. Note: HP is a New Zealand-registered company, so can be used in the NCEA exams as a business example.

Hewlett Packard Enterprise will build upon HP's leading position in servers, storage, networking, converged systems, services and software. HP Inc. will be the leading personal systems and printing company with a strong roadmap into the most exciting new technologies like 3D printing and new computing experiences.

Why?

Meg Whitman, Chairman, President and Chief Executive Officer of HP:

"The decision to separate into two market-leading companies underscores our commitment to the turnaround plan. It will provide each new company with the independence, focus, financial resources, and flexibility they need to adapt quickly to market and customer dynamics, while generating long-term value for shareholders. In short, by transitioning now from one HP to two new companies, created out of our successful turnaround efforts, we will be in an even better position to compete in the market, support our customers and partners, and deliver maximum value to our shareholders."

The NCEA Business Standards require students to demonstrate knowledge of a New Zealand-registered business in a number of areas, including change management, supply chain issues, quality management, societal expectations of business, changes in the global business environment, cultural intelligence, etc.

For this case study, the focus will be on HP NZ, which is more familiar, its printers, laptops, desktops, etc. are found throughout New Zealand and the world.

Change management: as you would expect, the split of a major company into two components meant significant changes across the business, including the following:

1	2	3	4	5
New email addresses for approximately 260,000 employees of Hewlett Packard Enterprise, as HP Inc. retained existing email format.	New logo for Hewlett Packard Enterprise, as HP Inc. retained the existing logo.	New contracts for every employee with the new legal entities.	Possible changed reporting channels as employees were allocated to each new company.	New IT infrastructrure for each new company, including finance, HR, database management, supply chain, etc. In many cases these could be cloned, but the legal requirement is for completely separate systems and no sharing of data.

How was this to be accomplished?

HP decided very early on to ensure employees were involved with the change process, including extensive communications by the leadership team by video and email. While the change into two separate businesses was being undertaken, the company still needed to maintain its supply of existing and new products to the market and build profitability, market share, quality and innovation to attract investors into the two new companies in November 2015.

Questions for Level 3 Business Studies: refer to www.HP.com, particularly:

- What will happen to innovation from the single company to now two smaller, separate businesses? Justify your response after researching HP.

  _____

  _____

  _____

- Who are the leaders at HP? Who is Meg Whitman and Dion Weisler, and what role might they have on corporate culture?

  _____

  _____

  _____

- What has been stated as the strategic direction of the company HP?

  _____

  _____

  _____

  _____

  _____

 ISBN: 9780170352598

- Where is HP NZ located? Who is the New Zealand-based leader of HP in NZ?

- Describe what some of the company values might be?

- Research how HP dealt with intellectual property (IP). How did patents from 10+ years ago become 'owned' by the two new companies? Hint: see HP Labs.

- HP has factories all around the world, including the USA, China, Germany. What supply chain issues might the company face?

- What ethical issues might HP encounter operating in so many countries?

- How would HP deal with technology changes — leading or following? What strategy is HP taking on new technology going forward from now?

- Who are the major competitors to HP? Name three, but be careful in classifying a competitor. Does the competitor compete in a single area (such as printers) or across a range (laptops, printers, desktops, tablets, etc.)?

- What does HP look for in new employees? See HP Careers.

  _____

  _____

  _____

- Is HP a multinational? And what opportunity does it bring to New Zealand? What threats to local manufacturing (if any)?

  _____

  _____

  _____

- What societal expectations are on HP, and how does it interact with the community? See the HP website on Living Progress.html, particularly across the headings Human, Economic and Environmental.

  _____

  _____

  _____

- Would trade agreements impact on HP? Consider the proposed free trade agreement TPP (Trans Pacific Partnership). Would New Zealand benefit, HP benefit, USA benefit?

  _____

  _____

  _____

- Research HP's financial performance over the past four years — how have economic changes, environmental pressures and political unrest affected HP?

  _____

  _____

  _____

- Investigate HP's commitment to warranty requirements for products across the world. What standard would they need to operate in terms of quality to be a global supplier?

  _____

  _____

  _____

ISBN: 9780170352598

Where can I learn more?

Option 1:

Young Enterprise Trust — inspiring young entrepreneurs

How we can help young people thrive as entrepreneurs? What does it mean to be enterprising? There are many ways that people define the word 'enterprise'. For some, it has connotations of innovation and endeavour, while others think of the 'number-eight wire' mentality.

At Young Enterprise Trust (YET), an enterprising person is someone who:

- is a creative and innovative thinker
- can recognise opportunities, and
- is willing to take risks.

Enterprising people lead our business community, nurture our young people and support our most vulnerable. The organisation was created in the 1980s to give school students access to authentic learning experiences.

In 1980, YET piloted the Lion Foundation Young Enterprise Scheme (YES), before offering it nationwide in 1981.

YES is an experiential programme where secondary students set up and run a small business in the space of four school terms. They create a product or service and bring it to market. YES students learn about key aspects of business including business planning, raising startup capital, prototyping, production, marketing and sales.

For more details, see www.youngenterprise.org.nz.

case study

Be a change-maker — Aparima College, Southland

Jessica Black wanted to galvanise the other students into action at Aparima College in Southland. In 2014, she managed a Young Enterprise company that produced an environmentally friendly and sustainable liquid seaweed concentrate made from seaweed collected from a local beach in Riverton. Having lived and helped on her family farm all her life, 17-year-old Jessica saw the importance of kaitiakitanga, the guardianship of resources. She gained consent from the local iwi for gathering a trailer-load of seaweed, soaked the ingredients in recycled barrels,

and, six months down the line, sold the seaweed concentrate in recycled plastic milk containers. Jessica named the product 'SeaChange', partly as a pun on its marine origins, but also because she really wanted to see her product make a positive change in the local community. She teamed up with two other students from farming families, and marketed the product to local gardening groups, elderly residents of the town who had no space for a compost heap in their own gardens, and at events such as Pet Day where children bought the product to enrich their gardens. Jessica's company gifted 25 percent of their profit to the QEII Environmental Trust to help with their important environmental work.

A change that Jessica was not expecting to see was the inspirational effect that running a YES company had on her and her fellow directors. As a team, Jessica's company suffered some rocky moments, and at times her fellow directors lacked motivation, but she persevered, continuously thinking of events and goals to inspire them. They won the Southland regional competition and went on to represent Southland at the national event. Jessica continued to sell the product after the wind-up of the company, and donated all the profit as startup capital for her 2015 Young Enterprise Company.

Option 2:

Enterprise in Action

Each year, 80 Young Enterprise students representing their regions converge on Massey University's Albany campus for one of Young Enterprise Trust's biggest events of the year: Enterprise in Action (EIA).

EIA is made up of two business challenges over 24 hours — a global problem-solving challenge and an export strategy challenge.

EIA provides an opportunity for students to meet like-minded young entrepreneurs and to be mentored by business professionals from high-profile companies such as Air New Zealand, HP and Spark. It is a weekend of challenges, competition, networking, teamwork, presentations and not much sleep: it's all huge fun.

At the end of the weekend, six students are chosen to represent New Zealand in Asia at the FedEx/JA International Trade Challenge to create a market entry strategy for a new product in a designated country. In 2014 the challenge was: 'Create a cohesive market entry strategy plan for a beauty product/service, which also addresses a social issue in your target country: Kenya.'

The winning team pitched a waterless face-wash solution called Eye Care, which addresses the trachoma disease that is prevalent among Kenyans, while not burdening users with the need for clean water. They took home a trophy each and a cash prize of $US4,000. In 2015, the New Zealand team once again took first place in this prestigious competition.

Option 3:

Business Boot Camp

Developed by David Farquhar with partners Jeff and Loren Stangl from Massey University in 2014, the Business Boot Camp is held at Massey University in Albany in the first-term holidays each year around April/May. The Camp involves approximately 75 students giving up a week of the break to immerse themselves in all things business, including visiting major businesses in Auckland and hearing direct from business leaders as to what makes them successful.

The range of activities includes a chef's team challenge, business games, business theatre, and a formal business lunch each day themed and presented by a key sponsor. There is a balance of hard skills, such as finance, and soft skills, such as networking/public speaking, with any formal lecture only being of one-hour duration to maximise impact and variety.

Key sponsors of the event are HP, Massey University, BNZ and NZX.

While the aim is to develop a passion for business, it is also an opportunity to build networking skills among the students attending who come from a range of schools and backgrounds. Many of the students have been involved in Young Enterprise and have therefore developed their own businesses, plus a high proportion are leaders within their schools in sports, academics or cultural activities.

Students leave the Business Boot Camp with developed public-speaking skills, confidence in developing business ideas, and an understanding of the real world of business. Plus they each gain 74 friends as potential future business leaders.

ISBN: 9780170352598

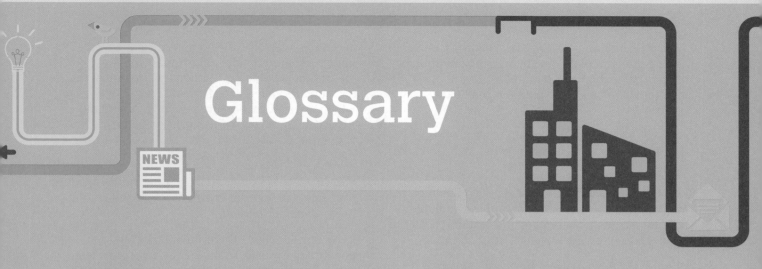

Glossary

Accountability   Being answerable/explaining yourself to the person who has delegated responsibility to you.

Asset   Something of value that a business owns, e.g. cash, buildings, vehicles, stock, accounts receivable.

Authority   The responsibility and power to control business decisions and issue instructions down the organisation.

Autocratic leadership   Where the leadership decides alone, often due to lacking trust in subordinates or to speed decision-making.

Big Data   A collection of data from traditional and digital sources inside and outside a business that represents a source for ongoing discovery and analysis.

Boom   Period of rapid economic expansion resulting in higher GDP, lower unemployment and rising asset prices.

Budget   A financial plan for the future, which forecasts future earnings and future spending, usually over a 12-month period.

Business cycle   The fluctuations in economic activity that an economy experiences over a period of time. The business cycle is basically defined in terms of periods of expansion or recession.

Business expansion   Growing the size of a business either internally or externally.

Business objectives   The aims or targets that a business is striving to work towards.

Capacity   The maximum amount of output a business can produce with available resources.

Capital   The money invested into a business by the owners.

Centralised   Where all major decisions are made by either one person or a few senior staff at the top of the hierarchy rather than being delegated to junior managers or other locations.

Chain of command   The vertical line of authority. Orders or instructions pass along this line through layers of hierarchy.

Change management   The planning, implementing, controlling and reviewing of the movement of an organisation from its current state to a new one, while minimising resistance to the change through the involvement of key players and stakeholders.

Citizenship   For a business, citizenship refers to how it interacts with the wider community - locally, nationally and internationally.

Code of Conduct   A code of practice/set of guidelines for staff to operate under, covering issues such as bribery, theft, treatment of customers and information.

Collective bargaining   When negotiations are between more than one union and/or employers.

Consumer behaviour   The process by which individuals search for, review, choose, buy, consume and dispose of goods and services, in satisfaction of their needs and wants.

Contingency plan   A plan that prepares an organisation's resources for unlikey events, including natural disasters, disruptions to supply chain, or IT failures.

Continuous improvement   A policy of constantly measuring performance and developing methods to improve. To never accept that there is no room for improvement. Refer *Kaizen*.

Copyright   Legal monopoly that protects published or unpublished original work from unauthorised duplication without due credit and compensation.

Corporate culture   The values, attitudes, beliefs and behaviours that contribute to the environment of an organisation and influences how people interact with each other both internally and externally.

Corporate Social Responsibility   Considering the welfare of all stakeholders when decisions are made.

Cultural intelligence   The ability of a business to adapt to new markets, have an appreciation of the cultural mix of its customers and workforce, and to build a sustainable business across cultures.

Culture   The values and norms within an organisation.

Decentralised   Where decision-making authority is shared out to other staff to empower them to make decisions.

Delegation   Handing authority for decision-making and task-setting to an employee down the organisation structure. Note that the final responsibility will still rest with the delegator.

Democratic leadership   Where the business is run in consultation with input from staff. Often characterised by high levels of delegation and discussion by leaders to staff on decisions made.

Demographics   The physical characteristics of a population such as age, sex, marital status, family size, education and occupation. For example, a town's demographics suggest whether certain restaurants will do well there.

Diversification   The reduction in risk of one market or product by developing new products or markets.

Economic growth   The value of the goods and services produced within a country in a given time period (usually a year).

Economic sustainability   The ability of a business to support a defined level of economic production indefinitely. The development of industrial and natural resources that meets the needs of the present economy without compromising the ability of future generations to meet their needs in a similar manner.

Economies of scale   The reduction in long-run average costs as a result of expanding the scale of production.

Efficiency   How effectively a business is using its resources. Measured by output per hour or per worker.

Enterprise culture   Being enterprising involves being prepared to take risks and to 'think out of the box' in developing solutions to problems. The term culture refers to the typical way of behaving within an organisation or in society as a whole. An organisation with an enterprise culture is one where people are imaginative and creative, rather than being reluctant to take risks.

Ethics   The set of moral principles that a business may establish for that business to operate under. Refer *Code of Conduct*.

Export incentives   Government incentives to encourage exports, such as financial, tax or legal incentives designed to encourage businesses to export certain types of goods or services.

External factors   Factors that affect businesses from outside the organisation itself that the busiess has no direct control over, e.g. tax rates.

External growth   Business growth achieved by taking over or merging with another business.

Financial information   Reporting and production of financial accounts so that users can have an accurate view of the firm's financial position and can make informed decisions and plans.

Fiscal policy   The government policy involving raising revenue (e.g. taxes, fees) and its expenditure (education, social welfare).

Free trade   The unrestricted buying and sale of goods and services between countries without the imposition of barriers such as duties, tariffs and quotas.

Globalisation   Globalisation is the worldwide movement towards economic, financial, trade and communications integration. It implies the opening of local and nationalistic perspectives to a wider outlook of an interconnected and interdependent world with free transfer of capital, goods and services across national frontiers to improve standards of living.

Gross Domestic Product (GDP)   Represents the country's income earned from production in that country. For example, New Zealand's GDP includes income from production carried out by New Zealanders and by foreign firms operating within New Zealand over a period of time.

Gross profit   The difference between the revenue from selling a good and the cost of buying it in.

Horizontal integration   The merging of businesses that produce the same product at the same stage of the production chain.

Human resources   A responsibility of management, e.g managing staff, recruiting, training, appraising. Previously called Personnel Department.

Import restrictions   Methods used to control goods coming into a country. Also called import controls, they include tariffs (import duties), import quotas that limit the total quantity of goods imported, and prohibition that prevents entry of illegal or harmful items.

Innovation   Bringing a new idea into being, such as a product for sale (product innovation) or a new way of producing something (process innovation).

Intellectual Property   Intellectual Property (IP) is an umbrella term used for human innovations and creativity that are capable of being protected under national law and international treaties. IP includes a diverse range of commercial assets from patents for new inventions through to copyright-protected artworks.

Invention   The creation of a new idea, product or process. Invention happens before innovation.

Kaitiakitanga   Responsibility for protecting resources for future generations, such as sustainable fishing or forestry.

Kaizen   A Japanese term meaning continuous improvement, based on small improvements being suggested and implemented often with little cost from workers' suggestions. Credited with the development of the Japanese car industry.

Laissez-faire leadership   Where the leader has very little input into the running of the business, leaving it to staff to make the decisions.

Layers of hierarchy   The number of layers or 'ranks' within an organisational structure, usually counted from the CEO to the shop floor staff member.

Leadership style   This can be democratic, autocratic, paternalistic or laissez-faire.

Lean production   Production where as few resources as possible are used: space, materials, stock, time and labour.

Lockout   When an employer prevents the workforce from getting to work, such as literally 'locking the gates'.

Manager   A staff member in charge of other staff and who has higher level responsibility in running an organisation. The manager will be accountable to the directors/shareholders for reaching targets.

Marketing   A management role to determine consumers' needs and wants and satisfying them, e.g. conducting market research, implementing marketing strategy, supervising marketing staff. The four Ps are: product, place, price, promotion.

Merger   When the managements and shareholders of two businesses agree to join together to form one business.

Monetary policy   Action taken through the Reserve Bank to vary the rate of interest or the supply of credit in the economy as a means of controlling inflation.

Multinational Corporation (MNC)   An enterprise operating in several countries but managed from one (home) country. Operations could include production, resource gathering, technical research facilities and assembly, such as Toyota or Fuji Xerox.

Net Present Value (NPV)   A calculation that compares the amount invested today to the present value of the future cash receipts from the investment.

Net profit   Net profit is gross profit less expenses.

New Zealand Trade and Enterprise (NZTE)   The Government's international business development agency.

Offshoring   When the activity the independent supplier is providing takes place overseas. For example, Chinese clothing made under licence to a New Zealand firm.

Operations management   The management of the supply chain function. Refer *Supply chain*.

Organisational chart   A diagram that illustrates the structure of an organisation including lines of authority and levels of hierarchy.

Organisational culture   The attitudes, decision-making, ethics and 'way of doings things' of an organisation.

Organisational hierarchy/structure   The levels of management and division of responsibility within an organisation.

Outsourcing   When a business uses independent suppliers rather than undertaking the activity themselves, e.g. hiring an accountant to process the firm's taxes or payroll.

Patent   Limited legal monopoly granted to an individual or firm to make, use and sell its invention, and to exclude others from doing so.

Paternalistic leadership   An autocratic-type style but with some discussion and input from staff, but with little delegation. The leader makes the decisions based on what he or she feels is best for the business. Similar to a traditional 'father to children' role.

Payback period   Refers to the period of time required to recover the funds expended on an investment. For example, a $1000 investment that returned $500 per year would have a two-year payback period. The time value of money is not taken into account.

PEST   Political, Economic, Social, Technological — a systematic method of evaluating influences on a business's external environment. Sometimes Technological will also include Environmental, Ethical and Legal — STEEPLE.

Primary sector   Business sector involved with agriculture, fishing and extraction industries such as mining, oil exploration.

Production   The making of goods and services, the output of a business.

Productivity   A measurement of the efficiency with which a firm turns production inputs into output.

Protectionism   The deliberate attempt to limit imports or promote exports by putting up barriers to trade.

Putake   The reason for being'— closely connected to the Quadruple Bottom Line, where the objectives of the business are more than just profit.

Quadruple Line Reporting   Triple bottom line (economic, social and environmental effects) plus cultural impacts.

Rangatiratanga   The exercise of leadership, authority, guardianship, and ownership rights; particularly focused on resource production, utilisation and management for current and future requirements.

Rate of return   The amount of time it will take to recover an investment. For example, if you invest $1000 and receive $150 in the first year of the investment, the rate of return is 15%, and you will recover the initial $1000 in six years and eight months.

Recession   Two consecutive quarters (six months) of negative growth in GDP.

Redundancy   When a job function is no longer required, and is not connected to an employee's performance or behaviour. Can be referred to as retrenchment.

Restructure   Reorganising the business to be more efficient. May result in redundancies.

Risk assessment   The attempt to identify and quantify the risks faced when undertaking a course of action.

Secondary sector   Business sector that manufactures products or is involved in construction, e.g. pet-food canning business, oil refining.

Stakeholders   Any individual or group who is interested in or directly affected by the activities of the business. The main stakeholders are employees, suppliers, shareholders, customers and the local community.

Strategy   A plan of action for the whole organisation that is designed to achieve a particular goal. Strategy occurs at the top level of an organisation and is distributed across the organisation. It is not a local plan for a branch, single-country, business unit or department.

Supply chain   The sequence of activities that converts raw materials into a product/service purchased by consumers.

Takeover   When one business buys out the owners of another business for control. Usually not by agreement. See *Merger*.

Tangible assets   Things that have a physical presence, such as machinery, cash, buildings.

Tariff   A tax imposed on an imported product into a country. Duty free means no tariff is charged, such as at the airport.

Tertiary sector   Business sector that provides services to consumers and other businesses, e.g. accountants, car washes.

Tikanga   The set of values that sets Māori business apart from other businesses, particularly businesses that operate solely to produce a profit for the owners/shareholders. These values include diversity, unity, spirituality, guardianship of resources and a sense of belonging.

Triple Line Reporting   Measurement and reporting of the economic, social and environmental effects of the business.

Tūranga   The foundation or positioning of the business. Why it has been formed – for what purpose is it in existence.

Unique selling point   The feature of a product or service that differentiates it from competitors, e.g. Marmite.

Vertical integration   When one business merges or takes over another business in the same industry, but at a different stage of production. For example, a glass maker buys a sand-mining operation to secure raw material supplies.